INVENTORS
AND THEIR BRIGHT IDEAS

by Dr Mike Goldsmith

Illustrated by Clive Goddard

Hippo

Scholastic Children's Books,
Euston House, 24 Eversholt Street,
London NW1 1DB, UK

A division of Scholastic Ltd
London ~ New York ~ Toronto ~ Sydney ~ Auckland
Mexico City ~ New Delhi ~ Hong Kong

Published in the UK by Scholastic Ltd, 2002

Text copyright © Dr Mike Goldsmith, 2002
Illustrations copyright © Clive Goddard, 2002

10 digit ISBN 0 439 98109 3
13 digit ISBN 978 0439 98109 5

Typeset by M Rules
Printed and bound by Bookmarque Ltd, Croydon, Surrey

14 16 18 20 19 17 15

CONTENTS

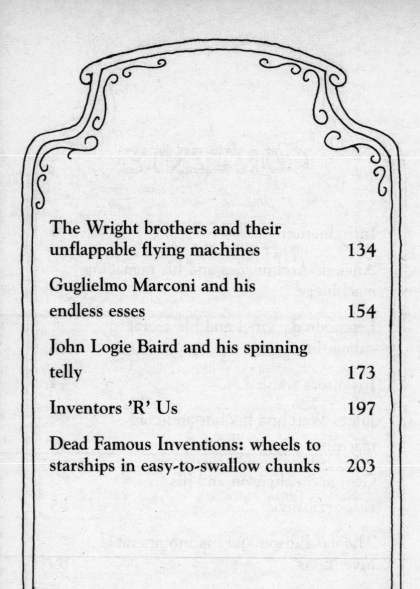

INTRODUCTION

If it wasn't for whoever it was who invented reading and whoever else it was who invented introductions, you wouldn't be reading this introduction now. It's a stunning thought, isn't it? Good old inventors – you can probably think of loads of them and the great things they invented.

JAMES WATT AND THE STEAM ENGINE!

GEORGE STEPHENSON AND THE TRAIN!

JOHN LOGIE BAIRD AND THE TELLY!

THE WRIGHT BROTHERS AND THE FLYING MACHINE!

EDISON AND THE LIGHT BULB!

MARCONI AND THE RADIO!

Everyone knows about them, don't they? But everyone's wrong! Lucky you bought this book really...

The thing is, dead famous inventors have got a bit of a tendency not to have done what they're famous for. This book is just full of surprises like that (not to mention a talking dog).

But you will find out who *did* invent all these great things, as well as why the people in this book really do deserve their fame – because there's more to being an inventor than being first to think something up.

SUCH AS?

Well, an inventor *can* be…
- 'the first person to think something up' – which would make Leonardo a really triffic inventor.

But they can also be…
- 'the person who made the first version of something' – like Thomas Edison.
- 'the first person to make something work really well so that everyone wanted one' – like Guglielmo Marconi.
- 'the first person to patent[1] something' – like Alexander Graham Bell.

In this book, 'inventor' can mean any of those things.

Between them, these inventors came up with a good chunk of the world's most important inventions. But not all of them. Some really brilliant things have unknown inventors – like wheels, clocks and pockets. Others were invented by teams of people, often taking decades or even centuries to get them right – like the computer, the

---

1. You'll find out all about patenting later on page 47.

spaceship or the piano (which took over 2,000 years and over 2,000 other inventions to perfect!). Because this book is about famous inventors, not famous inventions, these don't get a look in.

You'll also notice that the inventors in this book stop inventing somewhere around the 1930s. That's because from then on most inventions, like CDs, instant noodles and satellites, were thought up by big companies. But if you want to be an inventor yourself, don't worry – there are still people inventing marvellous things that make them rich and famous, and there's certainly plenty left to invent.

So read on and find out...
- Why the Roman Army was terrified of an old mathematician.
- Why miners used to dress up in rotting fish-skins.
- Who experimented with a disembodied human ear.
- Why elephants can't fly.
- What Frankenstein *really* invented.

To start with, let's go back a long way in time, to one of the greatest and oldest inventors of all. Only he didn't want to be one...

ANCIENT ARCHIMEDES AND HIS MENACING MACHINERY

Archimedes is not only very famous, he's also very dead. He lived over two thousand years ago. In those days, no one had got round to inventing much yet.

The problem with Archimedes being so incredibly ancient is that, though there are loads of stories about him, it's hard to know which are true. Apart from a few of his own writings, we often have to rely on copies of copies of books written by people who lived long after Archimedes but whose granny's uncle once met him at a party. Even Cicero, a Roman historian who did some proper research into Archimedes, lived over three centuries later. This all means that some of the things Archimedes is famous for probably never happened…

HE RAN NAKED DOWN A STREET SHOUTING 'EUREKA' BECAUSE HE'D INVENTED…ERM …STREAKING?

EUREKA!

But he still did a lot of amazing things, like…
• Launching a ship all by himself.
• Building a giant claw and using it to sink ships.
• Making a working model of the solar system.
And he was definitely one of the greatest mathematicians ever.

Startling sums

Maths was by far Archimedes' favourite thing to do: all his surviving books are about it, and he much preferred it to inventing. He probably wouldn't be famous as an inventor at all if the Romans hadn't tried to massacre everyone in his city.

Anyway… Archimedes was born in 287 BC in Syracuse, a seaside town in Sicily. His dad was an astronomer, and his family might have been related to the king, Hieron the Second. When he was a young man, Archimedes went off to Alexandria in Egypt to study. Alexandria was famous for two stunning things – a massive lighthouse called the Pharos, which was one of the seven wonders of the world[1], and an incredible library, which wasn't.

People from all over the place went to the library, and it contained all the knowledge of the world in the form of hundreds of thousands of texts, including – probably – plans of loads of inventions. Sadly it was burnt down three times over the centuries and now there's nothing left of it. The Pharos lasted longer but, after being damaged by an earthquake in AD 365 and another one in 1303, it finally collapsed in 1326.

The Alexandrians must have been dead impressed with Archimedes, because when he went back to Syracuse they asked him to keep sending them his mathematical discoveries. Archimedes was quite happy to do that – until he heard that some Alexandrians were passing off his theorems as their own. So next time he

1. And the only one that was actually any use.

sent his results, he put in a few false statements as well, so the sneaky Alexandrian mathematicians would get their sums wrong.

THE ALEXANDRIANS
ALEXANDRIA, EGYPT
TUESDAY, 265 BC

DEAR ARCHIMEDES,

HOPE YOU ARE KEEPING WELL. WE'RE FINE, THOUGH QUITE A LOT OF US HAVE DIED OF PLAGUE LATELY. STILL, MUSTN'T GRUMBLE. THANKS FOR THE SUMS – AMAZING STUFF! ALL THE OTHER CITIES CAN'T BELIEVE OUR YOUR PROOF THAT 2+2=5! IN FACT THEY ALL THINK ~~WE'VE~~ YOU'VE GONE NUTS! LITTLE DO THEY KNOW, EH, ARCHY? BY THE WAY, YOU DO SEEM TO HAVE LEFT A FEW LINES OUT OF YOUR PROOF. YOU COULDN'T SEND US ANOTHER COPY, COULD YOU? NO RUSH. WHENEVER. [STILL, NO TIME LIKE THE PRESENT, AS THE PHILOSOPHERS SAY!]

ALL THE BEST FROM YOUR PALS,
        THE ALEXANDRIANS

Back in Syracuse, Archimedes was spending so much time doing maths he often forgot to bathe or eat. When he did get round to having a nice oily bath there wasn't much point anyway, because he'd only write sums on himself, using grime and ashes from the fire.

Maths in those days meant geometry, and Archimedes thought it was such fun he even made a geometrical study of a popular game in which differently shaped pieces could be rearranged to form patterns. One of the many things that hadn't been invented yet was advertising – otherwise the game might have been called 'Sneeker' or 'Ker-pling'. Actually, its name means something like 'Stomach'. Which is odd really.

Anyway, Archimedes was really amazing at maths. He discovered the geometrical relationship between a sphere and a cylinder, which was rather clever and very handy but we haven't got time to find out about it now.

He also worked out a new way to estimate the value of π (the number of times the diameter of a circle can fit into its circumference – very popular with mathematicians, gardeners, architects, engineers and anyone else who uses circles), as well as coming up with a way of expressing very large numbers, which turned out to be really useful for later mathematicians (as well as for Archimedes himself, who worked out how many grains of sand it would take to fill the Universe – which turned out to be quite a few). And he devised the very first version of what is now called integration, which is a way of working out the area of a shape by dividing it up into lots of little bits of known area and adding them together. Almost any serious scientific maths now involves integration.

Macho machinery

But as well as all this (and even though he wasn't terribly keen on the idea), Archimedes did actually invent things too.

One of these inventions amazed everyone. It was a way of enormously increasing a person's strength – or so it seemed. It's said that, to convince people, Archimedes organized a public demonstration. A thick rope was attached to a huge, fully laden ship that was all ready to be launched, and Archimedes connected the other end to his invention, on the far side of the harbour. When his audience was in place, Archimedes began to pull on

a second rope connected to the other side of his machine, and the rope connected to the ship first tautened and then very slowly dragged the ship into the sea. Everyone was amazed. How could the machine have made him so much stronger?

Actually, it hadn't. The invention was an arrangement of pulleys, each of which worked like this:

Between the upper picture and the lower one, Archimedes has pulled out one metre of rope, but this only results in the ship moving half a metre. As you can see, this is bound to happen – it's the only way Archimedes' rope can stay the same total length (which is five metres – just add up the labelled lengths in the pictures). So the end of his rope moves twice as far as the ship's rope does: but the ship's rope pulls on the ship twice as hard as Archimedes pulls on his rope. It's a bit like using a claw-hammer to lever a nail out – you move your end a long way with a smallish force, while the claw-end moves a short distance with a lot more force.

By linking together lots of these pulleys, Archimedes could increase this effect many times – so he really could use his invention to move weights far heavier than he could have done otherwise. Machines like this were incredibly useful, especially for loading ships and for moving building materials.

One thing Archimedes *didn't* invent is something called the Archimedean Screw, which had been in use for some time in Egypt. He may have introduced it to Syracuse though. The Archimedean Screw is a water-pump, and it looked like this:

It works just like a corkscrew: as you rotate a corkscrew into a cork, bits of cork move up the length of the screw. The only difference is that the Archimedean Screw has a cylinder round it to stop the water falling out of the sides.

It's not surprising that Archimedes liked the Screw, since screws and cylinders were two of his favourite shapes, and it must have seemed as magical as his pulley-machine to people who didn't know how it worked, which was everyone. It came in very useful when one of King Hieron's big boats had been left out in the rain and had filled with water. Hieron asked Archimedes to give him a hand to empty it and Archimedes used an Archimedean Screw to do the job. The Screws probably became known by Archimedes' name because he went on about them so much. They're still used today, pumping all sorts of things, from blood (for people whose hearts aren't up to it themselves) to rainwater: they give a nice smooth flow and don't mind a few lumpy bits, unlike other sorts of pumps.

Archimedes, private investigator

Hieron also asked Archimedes to be his detective. He'd had a shiny new crown made for him by a goldsmith[1], and he'd given the goldsmith a big lump of gold to make it with. The crown weighed the same as the lump – but for some reason Hieron was suspicious.

Hieron wondered whether the crown was really made of pure gold – maybe the goldsmith had substituted some of the gold for silver and kept the rest for himself. Could Archimedes help?

He could indeed. After a bit of a think and a quick bath, he had it sussed. Supposedly, following the bath...

Archimedes had come up with a brilliant way of finding out whether the gold crown really was made of gold. He did it by realizing that, because gold is heavier than silver, a block of gold with the same volume as the crown must weigh the same as the crown, *unless* the crown was

1. No relation. Well, probably not.

made from a mixture of gold and silver. And he came up with a marvellously clever way of measuring the volume of the crown when he realized that the volume of water displaced by a submerged object is the same volume as the submerged object:

Clever, eh? Wouldn't you want to rush about naked after discovering that?

One experiment later…

For most of his life, Archimedes was almost certainly better known as a mathematician than an inventor. In fact, it wasn't until he was an old man that he spent very much time inventing. But then, thanks to the warlike Romans, he had to invent lots of things. Big, dangerous things.

Trouble with Romans

In Archimedes' time, Syracuse was in a bit of a tricky position. It was part of Greece, but not far off to the west was a powerful and bad-tempered place called Carthage. Up north, the Romans were, as usual, in a conquest-of-the-Earth kind of mood. They wanted to take control of Carthage, but Syracuse and other Greek cities were in the way. But the Romans weren't going

to let a little thing like that stop them and, when Archimedes was 23, war broke out between Carthage and Rome. To start with, Syracuse was on the side of Carthage, but the Romans offered some calm and reasoned arguments that convinced King Hieron that it would be less painful (not to mention bloody) for everyone if he supported them. So he did.

For a while, everything was peaceful – in a violent kind of way – until:

THE GREEK GAZETTE
218 BC

ELEPHANTS MAKE ROMANS PACK THEIR TRUNKS

For the first time in far too long, those rascally Romans have been defeated by a brave band of Carthaginian elephants, led over the Alps by General Hannibal. 'It was easy,' said Hannibal, 'the only dodgy moment was when the Romans cut off the bun supply.'

• Full story on page 3

POLL REVEALS SYRACUSE SPLIT ON ROMANS

Published today, a major poll of Syracusans shows strong opinions about Romans, with 48% ticking the 'They're really annoying, they're always getting drunk and shouting, not like those nice Carthaginians' box, while 52% said 'I like them, they might be animals, but they're *party* animals'.

• See page 6 for full details
• On page 7, win Hannibal's hat in our exclusive spot-the-elephant competition.

THE GREEK GAZETTE

217 BC

DEATH OF A KING

Exclusive eight-page colour pull-out section with photos of Hieron's funeral procession. Full report of Hieronymous' succession and five year plan on page 2.

On page 12, your chance to buy a limited-edition hand-crafted Hieronymous mug that will be yours to treasure for ever.

THE GREEK GAZETTE

216 BC

HIERONYMOUS ASSASSINATED BY PRO-ROMAN SYRACUSANS

Pro—Carthaginian Syracusans 'very irritated indeed'.

The Syracusans who supported the Romans had really gone a bit far this time. By assassinating the King of Syracuse, they sparked off a civil war. It didn't take long, though, before the war in Syracuse was over: the pro-Carthaginians had won. Rather unsurprisingly, the Romans weren't best pleased with them.

THE GREEK GAZETTE
214 BC

ROMANS SEND IN THE FRIGHTENERS

Roman Generals Appius Claudius Pulcher and Marcus Claudius Marcellus are on their way to besiege Syracuse, accompanied by a thousand troops and sixty battleships. Rumour has it that a charm offensive by the citizens of nearby Leontini got off to a bad start when Marcellus had them all beheaded.

THE GREEK GAZETTE
213 BC

'HIDE UNDER THE BED,' SYRACUSANS ADVISED

In another attack today, Marcus Claudius Marcellus attacked Syracuse with sixty battleships while his mate Appius Claudius Pulcher attacked the landward side of the city with his troops.

By this stage, Archimedes was 74 (which was ever so old in those days – most people were dead by 40) and probably wanted a quiet life. He certainly didn't want to be distracted from his sums by having to invent things. But Hippokrates and Epikydes, the latest rulers of Syracuse, were getting a little bit edgy, what with all the besieging and beheading and Latin and so on, and they decided they needed a bit of help.

So Archimedes (no doubt with a certain amount of muttering and tut-tutting) got to work building war machines. He made huge catapults that could hurl heavy rocks or massive beams of wood at people, special deadly crossbows called 'Scorpions' and, scariest of all, the 'Claw'. It's not quite certain how the Claw worked, but it was probably a special grappling iron that could be swung on to a ship by a crane…

When it had grabbed something, the Claw was jerked up, dragging the end of the ship with it. Then the Claw was suddenly released, and the ship would crash back into the sea and capsize. The Claw was also used to grab and drop individual Roman soldiers. Which served them right.

Some historians said that Archimedes also built huge mirrors of polished bronze to focus the Sun's heat on the ships and set them on fire. This seems unlikely: for one thing, the most reliable Greek historians don't mention it, and for another it would have taken an awful lot of mirrors. On the other hand, it's not impossible: experiments done since in the same harbour have shown that, if it was nice and sunny, it could have happened.

The Romans had no chance against Archimedes and his machines. They had some war machines of their own, including *sambucae*, which were scaling-ladders mounted on boats. But they were a bit pathetic compared to Archimedes' machines. He used them to drag the *sambuca* ships around until they were full

of water and all the sailors had swum away. It was all very annoying, but Marcus Claudius Marcellus (the leader of the Roman force) didn't lose his well-known sense of humour, saying:

Archimedes uses my ships to ladle sea-water into his wine-cups, but my sambuca band have been whipped out of the wine-party as intruders.

(Even though it doesn't make a lot of sense, it must be the sort of joke that had people laughing their heads off in those days – or maybe their heads came off if they *didn't* laugh.)

So the Romans had nothing to do but lay siege to Syracuse for the next two years. Finally, in 212 BC, when the Syracusans were having a big party, the Romans sneaked in and attacked them just as they were getting round to the trifle. Marcus instructed his soldiers not to kill Archimedes. He probably wanted him to build an automatic head-chopping-off machine.

When a Roman soldier found him, Archimedes was busily working on yet more diagrams. He refused to leave his calculations until he was finished, but the soldier had no time for that sort of thing, and killed him. Marcus wasn't happy, but there wasn't a lot he could do, so he contented himself with stealing Archimedes' inventions instead. One of these was a globe showing the positions of the stars, which Marcus gave to a temple in Rome. Another was a mysterious metal object, which so amazed Marcus that he kept it for himself. It was probably a moving mechanical model of the solar system: Cicero said that only a god-like being could have made such a thing. Cicero also tracked down Archimedes' tomb. A lot of the inscription had worn away by then, but a diagram of a sphere within a cylinder could still be seen.

ARCHIMEDES
THAT WAS YOUR LIFE

TOP INVENTIONS:
- compound pulley
- war machines
- model of the solar system

ALSO DEAD FAMOUS FOR:
being one of the greatest mathematicians ever

LEONARDO DA VINCI AND HIS SECRET SUBMARINE

Leonardo da Vinci invented the submarine, the glider and the tank five hundred years ago. And ... the first submarine was built in 1620, the first manned glider flew in 1849, and the first tanks were used in the 1910s.

HUH?

Exactly. Most of Leonardo's inventions were lost and had to be reinvented all over again centuries later.

It was all because Leonardo was a Renaissance Man. The Renaissance was a period in which Ancient Greek manuscripts, full of brilliant ideas, were brought to Italy. Everyone was *very* impressed and suddenly they got into all sorts of arts and the odd bit of science too. The idea of being a Renaissance Person was that you should know about all subjects – so ideally people didn't specialize in being scientists or writers or synchronized swimmers – they were annoyingly good at *everything*.

It was a good scheme, if tricky, but Leonardo had it sussed. In fact he was probably *the* Renaissance Man: he was one of the greatest painters ever; he drew maps; he made sculptures; he looked at the stars; he composed and performed music on instruments he invented and built himself; he studied rocks; he designed buildings – and even towns; he drew plants and fossils; he cut people up without spilling a drop of blood… (It's OK, they were dead. Which is just as well, since he also injected wax into their hearts and brains so he could make nice moulds of them.)

Leonardo was also really good-looking, ever so athletic, had amazing eyesight and was very strong indeed – he's supposed to have bent horseshoes with one hand. And he was a very kind bloke, a vegetarian who bought caged birds so that he could let them go.

MY HERO!

And, of course, he was an inventor.

Being Renaissance Man meant that Leonardo was *really* busy. He kept lots of notebooks, full of stunning ideas and brilliant illustrations, but he never got round to sorting them out and getting them published. Also, he was a bit concerned people would steal his ideas, or use them to kill each other. And he was often on the move. So while he was alive lots of his inventions were known only to him. After he was dead, his papers were scattered round the world, and most of the people who got hold of them were artists (because the idea of being Renaissance People had gone out of fashion by then). So his more sciency stuff was ignored. This happens even now – books about Leonardo tend to concentrate wholly on his art, which would probably have got on his nerves.

Jet-propelled germs

Leonardo was born near Vinci in Tuscany in 1452. We don't know much about his early life, but we do know that he grew up in an exciting but unsettled time. Italy was divided into five main areas, each dominated by a big city: Rome, Florence, Milan, Venice and Naples. The areas were controlled mostly by ruthless families – Leonardo worked for two of them, the Borgias and the Medicis. Although they were, by and large, horrible, they were into art. They were also, generally speaking, at war with each other, as well as with Turkey and France. So they liked artists and they liked people who could build them weapons. Leonardo could do both, so they liked him a lot.

To begin with, Leonardo *was* more into art than science. In 1469 he was taken on at the workshop of Verrocchio, a famous artist. It's said that Leonardo helped Verrocchio finish a portrait, by painting a head. Verrocchio said…

Well maybe. Anyway, Leonardo was a great artist. He drew rocks and water and animals and people, and he once terrified his dad by painting a monster and setting it up in a darkened room with a light shining on it.

Leonardo was gay, and homosexuality was then treated as a crime, punishable by being burnt at the stake. He was anonymously accused of being gay in 1476 and, though the charge was dismissed, it was one reason why he left Florence for Milan soon after.

By this time he was already at least as interested in science and engineering as art, and he wrote a letter to Ludovico Sforza, ruler of Milan, listing all the amazing things he could invent to help him with whatever war he happened to be having just then – things like indestructible bridges and stone-throwing machines. He mentioned he could paint a bit too. And sure enough, in 1482, Ludovico took him on … as a lyre player. Luckily, he could do that as well!

Being a lyre player didn't stop Leonardo inventing, and the fact he was really into peace didn't stop him thinking up a lot of weapons of war:

1. Only he said it in fifteenth-century Italian.

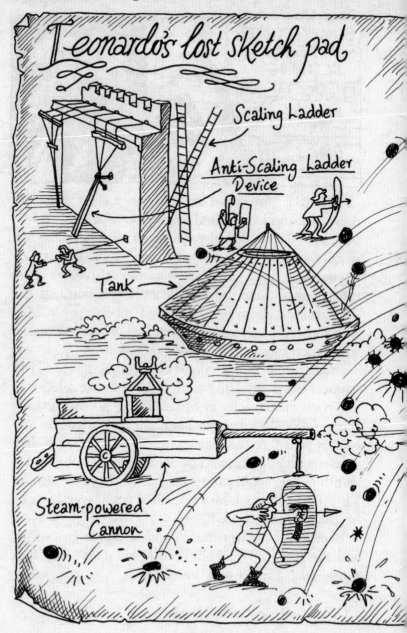

Leonardo's lost sketch pad

Scaling Ladder

Anti-Scaling Ladder Device

Tank →

Steam-powered Cannon

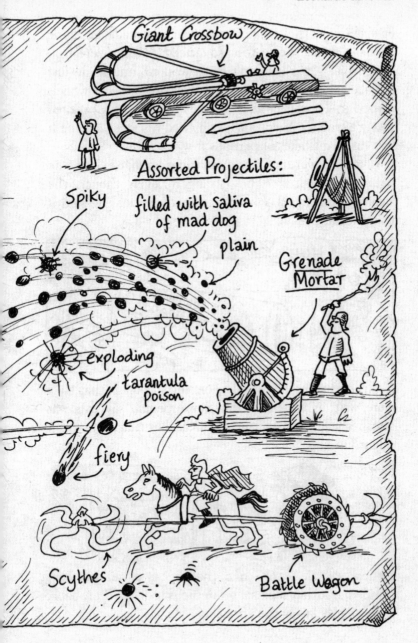

Giant Crossbow

Assorted Projectiles:

Spiky

filled with saliva
of mad dog

plain

Grenade
Mortar

exploding

tarantula
poison

fiery

Scythes

Battle Wagon

Few, if any, of these inventions were ever made, let alone used – some were too advanced, some were too expensive, some wouldn't have worked, and some just seemed too weird. The tank really *was* weird – its wheels turned in opposite directions. Maybe Leonardo wanted to lay a trap for anyone who pinched his ideas, maybe it was just a mistake, or perhaps it was a joke.

Like all inventors, not everything Leonardo came up with was original – but strangely, even though the steam-cannon probably was Leonardo's idea, he said it was Archimedes'.

An odd thing about all Leonardo's notes is that they were written back-to-front. Some people say this was another way of protecting his ideas, but that seems a bit unconvincing.

Others say he wrote like that because he was left-handed, but that seems a bit dubious too. We'll probably never really know the answer.

Is it a bird? Is it a plane? No, it's ... Renaissance Man!

To begin with, Leonardo's inventions were just ideas, not thought out in a lot of detail – he didn't yet worry about the science behind them. But in the 1480s, he started to look beneath the surface of things, by dissecting dead animals, especially birds. One of his other fascinations started about then too – the idea of conquering the air.

Leonardo's lost sketch pad.

1485

Had this brilliant idea today when I was painting the ceiling. I was thinking about how clever Archimedes was and how useful the Archimedean screw is for pumping water, when I thought – why not use it to pump air instead!

I could really fly with a thing like that –

up and up and up, miles above the land. And the rocks. And church steeples. And ... Hmmm. Maybe I'd better invent a ...

Leonardo's parachute was, like a lot of his inventions, a great idea and one that's been shown to work. (Though it needed a bit of modification to work properly – parachutes need a hole in the top or they swing wildly from side to side on the way down.)

Leonardo's helicopter design was one of his few inventions that had some real influence: though it was forgotten for centuries, it did inspire Igor Sikorsky to build the first successful helicopters in the 1940s. But it wasn't the first helicopter to be devised – as long ago as 1325, there were toy ones around, though they were based on windmills rather than Archimedean Screws. They didn't carry their own wind-up power like Leonardo's, which means that, if Leonardo made a working model – as it seems he did – it was the first flying machine in the world to carry its own power-source. But, like the parachute, it wouldn't have been much fun to fly in: the base would have spun round in the opposite direction to the air-screw. (Modern helicopters would do that too if it weren't for the secondary propellers on their tails.)

Leonardo only drew one sketch each of a helicopter and a parachute, but he drew lots and lots of other flying machines – most with flapping wings like those of the birds he studied. Most of the time, when Leonardo invented something, he was quite scientific about it, but he tended to get a bit carried away when he was thinking about flying, so some of his flying machines are a bit unlikely: like his flying boat with wings instead of oars. His most promising flying machines were glider-like inventions with no power source at all, but he didn't concentrate on them – he was much keener on the flappy kind. Some people say Leonardo put one or two to a real practical test…

Leonardo's last sketch pad
Spring 1495

Just got back from starting to paint The Last Supper. Decided to have another go at conquering the air. I'll make myself some wings like this:

and have a go. Or perhaps I'll let Ludovico have a try first. I'm sure he'd love to.

Move legs up and down furiously

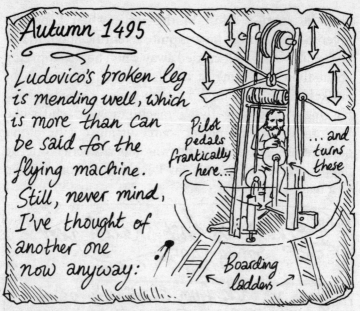

Autumn 1495

Ludovico's broken leg is mending well, which is more than can be said for the flying machine. Still, never mind, I've thought of another one now anyway:

Pilot pedals frantically here...

...and turns these

← Boarding ladders →

It's estimated that all the gubbins needed for this machine would weigh 300 kg, and it was all supposed to be lifted up by a man turning wheels, and pedalling. Very very fast.

Sadly, Leonardo's flying machines had no chance, especially with the heavy materials which were all he had available. Leonardo's big problem (which affected a lot of his other inventions too) was that there were no handy sources of power available – no electric motors, no petrol engines, no fuel-cells. All he had was human muscle, horse power and very basic forms of steam power. He used water power from rivers for several of his other inventions, but rivers aren't very suitable for flying with, and nor are horses (they always eat the in-flight magazines).

Leonardo did come up with a way of propelling his flying-machines – a somewhat wacky one. The idea was that the pilot would turn a wheel which would bend a powerful bow, like a crossbow. When the bow was released it would drive the wings, making them flap briefly. After that the machine would crash, unless the pilot could wind up the bow really quickly again (and again and again).

Another problem with Leonardo's flying machines is that, despite all his studies of birds, he still got the basic idea of how they fly wrong – he thought they did it by beating their wings down and back, like someone doing the breaststroke. But they don't. So his flapping-wing machines would never have flown, even if he had had a good power-source for them. We'll find out the secret of human flight when we get to the Wright brothers.

Water-tight schemes

Leonardo might have stayed in Milan for ages, happily designing weapons and flying machines, but in 1499 the French invaded it. Leonardo fled to Venice, but that wasn't much better – they were getting ready for a Turkish attack.

Leonardo's lost sketch pad
1499

Monday – The citizens of Venice have asked me to protect them from the Turks. That's the trouble with being Renaissance Man – people are always asking for new war machines. Why can't they just be nice to each other?

Never mind. I've got a cunning plan to flood the river area to make it impassable. Then, not only will there be no war, they can build new factories powered by water mills and everyone will be rich and happy. They'll love the idea.

<u>Thursday</u>. They hate the idea.

Oh well, back to the drawing board...

Diving bell

Mobile ram boat

Floats for walking on water

Air supply

Goggles

Turkish ship

Webbed gloves

Ship sinking drill

Flippers

Submarine

These marine schemes were almost as much fun for Leonardo as flying machines, since he was as fascinated with water as he was with flight. Though none of them were actually used, Leonardo was soon being employed full-time as an engineer by Venetian boss Cesare Borgia and travelling around with him. Even in those days when there were lots of vicious rulers about, Cesare was especially nasty. Leonardo turned a blind eye to it for a while, but when Cesare pretended to forgive some people who'd conspired against him, then invited them round for dinner and had them strangled, Leonardo had had enough. He went back to Florence where he helped the Florentine army to attack Pisa by planning a canal to divert the river Arno so Pisa would dry up. Luckily for Pisa the banks of the canal burst and the water returned to its original course.

A rather robotic Renaissance

In about 1503, Leonardo painted the most famous painting ever, the 'Mona Lisa'.

Four years later he was on the move once more, this time back to Milan, at the invitation of the French King, Louis XII, who ruled over the area at the time.

Leonardo was still fascinated with analysing things as well as inventing them. As he said:

> *Although human ingenuity makes various inventions, corresponding by various machines to the same end, it will never discover any inventions more beautiful, more appropriate or more direct than nature, because in her inventions nothing is lacking and nothing is superfluous.*

So he started to investigate the machine-like nature of the human body by dissecting people. The heart was a particular problem. Once out of the body, it tended to collapse into a squidgy mess. So Leonardo injected wax into the hearts of corpses and used the moulds to make plaster casts. He made amazing drawings of the heart, but didn't realize what it actually was – a pump to keep the blood circulating.

As usual, war interrupted Leonardo's work and when the French were driven from Milan in 1512, he realized it was time to move yet again – this time to Rome, where he worked for the new pope Giuliano de Medici, who gave him a workshop and some assistants. He didn't get on with them though – he thought they were stealing his ideas. They also killed birds, which was guaranteed to annoy him. But at least some of the inventions he came up with then a) weren't weapons and b) were actually used. One of these was a clever screw-cutting machine, which was in use for the next four hundred years or so. He also built an automatic weighing machine, a new type of water-clock and an instrument to measure humidity – all too far ahead of their time to catch on: like any inventions, they couldn't succeed until there was a really obvious need for them. By the time there was such a need, they'd been forgotten and had to be re-invented. But if things had been a little bit different, the sixteenth century might have been a lot more modern:

And who knows what the 21st century would be like!

Luckily, Leonardo didn't take things too seriously – in fact, he was a bit of a practical joker. When he was employed to invent ways to kill people he didn't have much chance for a giggle, but now things were a bit more peaceful, he had fun doing things like inviting friends round and inflating a bull's intestines with bellows until they filled the room they were in and everyone was all squeezed up in the corner. He also made inflatable animals that flew through the air, and disguised his pet lizard as a monster to frighten people.

All was peace and practical jokes until 1515 when Louis XII died. His energetic successor, François I, aged 20, won back Italian areas lost by Louis, and then called for peace talks at Bologna with Leo X. For the occasion, Leonardo made 'a lion which walked several steps and then opened its breast, and showed it full of lilies'. Unfortunately, no one knows exactly how this lion worked, though presumably it was a type of automaton – a robot-like machine, full of clockwork which made it move like a living thing. It wasn't Leonardo's only robotoid invention: he also invented a suit of armour that could stand up and sit down by itself, which must have *really* made people jump.

Leonardo's last move was in 1516, when he went to France, to work for François I. There, he invented an amazing prefabricated castle full of fountains, halls (all on the ground floor in case the floors collapsed), and toilets with automatically closing doors.

Leonardo never gave up on flying. Near the end of his life he made a real breakthrough:

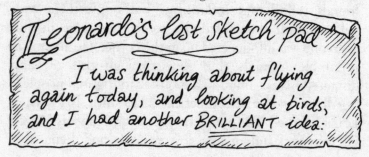

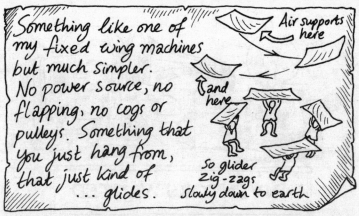

Something like one of my fixed wing machines but much simpler. No power source, no flapping, no cogs or pulleys. Something that you just hang from, that just kind of ... glides.

Air supports here

and here

So glider zig-zags slowly down to earth

Leonardo's hang-glider could really have worked, since it needed no power source. But he was too old by then to develop it: he died in 1519 at the age of 67. His ideas and inventions could have changed the world, but almost all his works were lost to science for 200 years. Two-thirds of them are still missing.

LEONARDO DA VINCI
THAT WAS YOUR LIFE

TOP INVENTIONS:
- flying machines
- war machines
- submarines and diving equipment

ALSO DEAD FAMOUS FOR:
being one of the greatest artists ever

INVENTORS WANTED

Both Archimedes and Leonardo were born well before their time. In their days, inventing was a strange and unusual thing to do, and people thought of inventors as rather nutty magicians (in fact some of them – like the inventor of one of the first robots – were tried as witches). The lack of power sources – especially portable ones – meant that whole areas of technology were just impossible, and without a means of mass-production, it wasn't easy for a new invention to catch on. Also, there just wasn't much need for inventions to take the drudgery out of life, because the people with the power didn't have to drudge anyway – they had slaves or servants to do it for them!

But then, in 1649...

Lots of things happened after this, but as far as inventors are concerned, the big change was that the upper classes, who had no interest in technology, lost some of their power, and there was more cash about for slightly lower-class people to spend on improving farming techniques. This, together with some nice hot summers, led to more food, and that meant…

So the population grew.

Meanwhile, Britain was building a big trading empire with its powerful navy, so there was yet more money about and there was a demand for goods to spend some of this money on: for ships to do more trading, for weapons to conquer more of the world, for houses for all the extra people to live in and for transport systems to move the people and materials and food and goods around. All this meant that people needed new technology, and that meant…

And the inventors came up with stacks and stacks of amazing new machines and techniques. For instance…

Also around this time, many countries started to organize patent systems. A patent is a bit of paper issued by a government that gives an inventor the exclusive right to make and sell their invention. That meant that inventions couldn't be copied so easily, and their creators had the chance to make a bit of cash from them, which is always nice.

Also, more people could read, and there were scientific societies and technical journals around, which meant more people were clearer about technical problems, and better equipped to solve them. Some people even started to learn a little bit of science at school, and the grip of religion – which tended to be anti-scientific[1] – started to weaken slightly. Suddenly, everyone loved inventors, because the Industrial Revolution had arrived.

1. When the fork was invented in 1000, the Church banned it because it stopped people using their God-given fingers to eat with.

Leonardo's quite right – though the Industrial Revolution was the start of the modern world, it was very bad news for a lot of people. Of course, there had always been poor people, but now their lives were more miserable than before: millions of them were crammed into rat-filled slums, grim factories, and horrible mines.

The Industrial Revolution was also the start of big-scale pollution that went more or less unchecked until the 1970s. Anyway, for better or worse industrialization had arrived, and the next couple of chapters are about two of its most important creators.

JAMES WATT AND HIS HOT-AND-COLD MACHINE

James Watt was a bit nervous of things that went BANG. And he decided to do something about them. In so doing he helped to start the Industrial Revolution and changed all our lives for ever. What James *didn't* do was invent the steam engine – that had been done over 1,500 years earlier in Greece, and several major improvements had been made to it by the time James came along. What he did was to change steam engines from clonky, wasteful things only good for a few jobs, into powerful, relatively efficient machines that were good at all sorts of stuff. Before we get on to that though, and find out more about James himself, let's have a quick look at steam engines before James sorted them out, and find out why anyone wanted them in the first place.

A brief hissstory of steam

The steam engine was invented in about AD 50 by an Ancient Greek bloke called Hero. He invented lots of steam-powered things, from singing birds to tootling horns. He called his steam engine an aeolipyle, and it was a sphere pushed round by steam-jets.

So there we go, the steam engine. That was easy, wasn't it? The Ancient Greeks were now free to invent steam railways, steam cars, steam ships, steam irons ... but they didn't. They just made steam toys for a giggle, or to impress their friends. The thing is, they had plenty of slaves to drag things about for them, row boats and do the ironing. They just weren't into technology. In fact, as we saw with Archimedes, they were a bit sneery about it and thought it wasn't a patch on a really juicy bit of thinking.

Later on, when people didn't have slaves so much, they relied on the power of the wind or water for doing things. Wind and water are fine for some things, like grinding corn or moving sailing ships – but they're not ideal. For one thing, they're not very portable – imagine having a wind-powered torch or a Walkman driven by a water-wheel. Also they're a bit unreliable: water does sometimes dry up or freeze (or drown you) and it's not *always* windy (unless you're carrying a bowl of confetti to school – which is why no one does, of course).

As we saw, this was a real problem for Leonardo, who would have loved a nice power source. He did suggest using steam power, but only to make a cannon go BANG. Which brings us back to James Watt again. Or it will in a minute.

In 1698 Thomas Savery patented a simple but quite clever type of steam thing. It wasn't really an engine though, more of a pump. It was quite handy – when it didn't explode that is, which it tended to do when the steam got too hot and pressed too hard on the insides of the boiler. Thomas called it: *A New Invention for Raiseing of Water and occasioning Motion to all sorts of Mill work by the Impellent Force of Fire* or *The Miner's Friend* for short, because it was supposed to keep mines nice and dry. The miners probably didn't feel all that matey about it though.

A bit later, in 1712, Thomas Newcomen built a really good sort of steam engine:

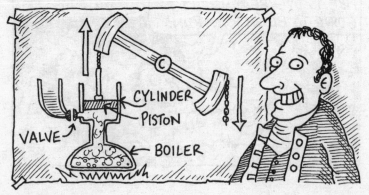

This was still only used for pumping water, but it worked fairly well, so everyone was more or less happy with it, and lots of miners wanted one to keep their mines dry. But Newcomen engines did use masses of fuel and they weren't very powerful. Though this caused a *lot* of moaning and dratting, people didn't realize just how wasteful they were, because there wasn't really a science of steam engines in those days. Steam engineers only ever tried to make their machines bigger, not cleverer.

Fun with boiling water

Twenty-four years after the Newcomen steam engine was built, James Watt was born on 19 January 1736 in Scotland. And he wasn't happy. He was ill and weak and always had toothache. When he went to school (at age 11) he was bullied. But he was somewhat happier when he moved on to grammar school two years later, where he turned out to be good at maths. His dad – who was a carpenter – had given him some small tools, and he turned out to be good at making things too. Even then he was interested in steam, and his aunty is supposed to have told him off for messing about with the kettle. He was a nice, quiet boy on the whole, though he did give his friends massive electric shocks from time to time (all in the cause of science, of course).

James decided that making scientific instruments would be a great job. One of his relatives taught at

Glasgow University so in 1754, aged 18, James set off to go there and became an instrument-maker.

It's important to note at some point (and it might as well be now) that James was a really nice bloke. This was very handy because he wasn't much of a salesman. In fact, he was rubbish at it – unlike everyone else in this book. If an inventor can't sell his ideas, he's got no chance of being successful, let alone dead famous – unless, like James, he has some good friends to help him. One of his first friends was Robert Dick, who got him a job repairing scientific instruments. Unfortunately, this didn't last long and there was no one in Glasgow who could teach him how to become a full-time instrument-maker.

Robert reckoned London was the place for James, so that's where he went, accompanied by a distant relative called John. Because trains aren't invented until the next chapter, it was a very long journey, partly because the horses had two days off for a bit of rest and relaxation.

Robert sent James to a friend of his in London who was an instrument-maker. But the friend – also called James – though helpful to our James, couldn't get him a job, and nor could anyone else. The trouble was, no one was allowed to take him on unless he'd served a long apprenticeship, which he hadn't. He did find a vacancy eventually, but it wasn't what you'd call a dream job.

Contract of Employment

Hours: long
Conditions: grimy
Pay: minus £21 per year, no expenses paid
(The employee must pay his employer for the valuable experience the job will give him.)

But James took the job. He had to get other jobs to make money to pay for it, not to mention food and a place to live, so he just worked and worked and worked until he was ill. Then he went back to his family in Scotland, where Robert managed to find him another repairing-scientific-instruments job. It was only temporary, but while he was doing it, James made two more friends – John Robison and Joseph Black, who was a scientist. It was lucky James was so popular at the University – he still couldn't become an instrument-maker outside it, because he still didn't have an apprenticeship. So the University let him set up shop on its grounds.

At last James didn't have to work himself to death any more and had his chance to change the world. So he did.

Yet another of his many friends, John Anderson[1], brought James a model steam engine to repair. It was a Newcomen one of course.

When James was mending it, he had a chance to find out exactly how it worked, and he was soon sussing out how to improve the design. James was different from other steam-engineers of his day in that he didn't just tinker with engines, making them bigger, feeding them more fuel and swearing at them. Instead, he tried to understand them...

James was a proper scientist and he soon saw that there was a basic problem with the Newcomen engine that meant it was incredibly inefficient. This is why:

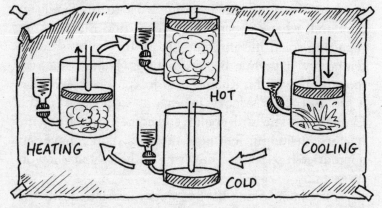

1. All James's friends had names beginning with J. Don't ask me why.

It was clever, but the cylinder had to be continually heated to over boiling point to change the water to steam and help push the piston-rod out, and then cooled again to change the steam back to water, so that air pressure could push it back in again. This repeated cooling process just wasted most of the heat that boiled the water. But James had a brilliant idea:

I'LL DO THE HEATING AND COOLING IN DIFFERENT PLACES!

So James built his own model with a separate condenser (a vessel cold enough to turn the steam to water). Then he could keep that cool and the cylinder hot and it would work with much less fuel. For a piston, James used an anatomist's syringe which was supposed to be for injecting wax into dead bodies (just like Leonardo used to use).

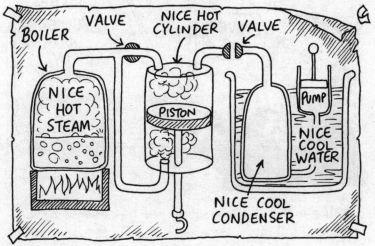

And it worked like this:

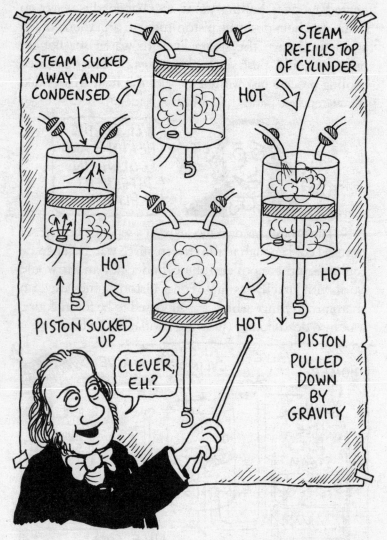

So that was easy then. James just had to wait for the money to roll in.

Eleven years later...

James waited ... and waited ... and waited ... for eleven years, while he was busy working as a land-surveyor, which he hated. Meanwhile, his steam engine just got rusty, dusty and a little bit musty. James might have waited for ever if it hadn't been for *another* friend, John Roebuck. He introduced James to Matthew Boulton[1], who turned out to be just the sort of friend James needed – a businessman. A few years after they first met they went into business together and James built a full-scale steam engine at last. In 1776 they showed it off to lots of engineers, mine-operators, businessmen and a reporter.

It was brilliant. It hissed and roared and went up and down and in and out and did all the things that steam engines do. It used a third of the fuel the Newcomen engines did, and everyone loved it. Watt knew that lots of people really needed it – especially the Cornish miners. (They had some very wet mines, but there was no local coal to feed steam engines with, which made Newcomen engines particularly unsatisfactory.)

It was nearly time for James to live happily ever after – but first he had to install one of his engines in Cornwall. Though they were well aware of the problems with the Newcomen engine, the miners didn't trust James or his machine to do any better. (And Richard Trevithick, who turns up again in the next chapter, had already tried to nick the plans of the machine, so that wasn't much of a start.) However, when James got it working, they all went wild with joy. Or at least nodded and grunted in a surly kind of way. He found that the more noise it made,

1. Don't ask me why his name didn't begin with J. It's a mystery.

the more they liked it, so he was careful to leave some nice rough bits on it that made satisfying squeals and graunches.

James's robotic brain

Matthew and James worked together happily for years. The money soon poured in, and James settled down to what he liked best: improving his steam engine. He increased its efficiency by using steam to move the piston both in and out, and worked out how to change the up-and-down motion of the piston to round-and-round motion.

And he invented something which was really important later, and very handy at the time too: *a thinking machine!* Well, sort of...

Dear J,

Sorry it's been so long since I last wrote, but I've been a bit busy with the Industrial Revolution and inventing new bits of steam engine. My latest one is brilliant for stopping steam engines going BANG. It looks like this:

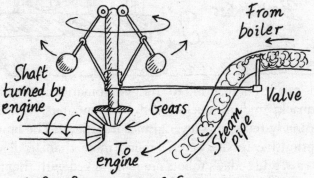

From boiler

Shaft turned by engine

Gears

Valve

Steam Pipe

To engine

What happens is, if the engine is going too fast, my invention spins round fast too, and the balls spin outwards. They're linked to a ring that slides up a vertical shaft. As it does it starts to close a steam valve. That cuts off some of the steam to the engine, which slows down.

If the engine is going too slowly, my invention slows down, the balls drop, the ring slides down and the valve opens wider, letting more steam through to the engine and speeding it up.

So it saves a person looking after the steam-engine's speed. I'm going to call it the Governor.

Hope you are well

Best wishes J.

This process of reacting to things automatically is called feedback, and is much loved by computers, central-heating systems and clever gizmos in general. The brains of primitive robots weren't much more than feedback systems, and today's robots are still packed with them.

Steamy science

James's steam engines changed the world because they were so much better than the Newcomen ones, but he'd never have succeeded if he'd just been a good mechanic. He was also a scientist, who analysed and solved practical problems logically. One of these problems was how the power of an engine should be measured.

Before steam engines, horses were often used in mines to drive pumps, so the power of a horse was a well-understood practical measure. It was a good scheme, since machines were doing horses' jobs, to compare their powers. But how could this be done? After a lot of study of the power of horses, James defined an imaginary standard horse and used it as a unit of power. These days, though, horsepower isn't used much as unit of power; more often we use one named after James: the Watt.

In 1800, when James was 64, the patent on his steam engine ran out so anyone could make one. He had loads of money by then, so that was no problem. But he reckoned it was about time he stopped working anyway, and just had fun. So he spent the next nineteen years happily retired in a big house he'd built, giving money away, gardening, travelling, reading and experimenting with new inventions like a sculpture-copying machine.

All sorts of people would come to ask him all sorts of things, from how to build more powerful engines to how to cure a smoky chimney. He was even asked weird questions like what to make really pliable artists' brushes out of and whether a perpetual motion machine was possible.[1] Luckily, despite all the fame and money and people telling him how brilliant he was, he was still a very nice bloke, so he patiently answered them all.

1. The answers were 'Rats' whiskers' and 'No'.

James kept a keen interest in the world around him – a world that was rapidly changing due to his own invention: in 1816, when he was 80, he had an outing on a newfangled steamboat and he couldn't resist tinkering with it to make it work better. New engines came along, using high-pressure steam, but he didn't hold with them. They were far too likely to go BANG.

Some people even wanted to make steam engines that could move around. James had considered them himself once but was soon sure it was a complete waste of time…

HMM…

GEORGE STEPHENSON

JAMES WATT
THAT WAS YOUR LIFE

TOP INVENTIONS:
- efficient steam engines with separate condensers
- new ways to make steam engines turn wheels
- the Governor: the first widely used 'feedback mechanism'

ALSO DEAD FAMOUS FOR:
inventing the old unit of power and having the new one named after him

GEORGE STEPHENSON AND HIS RISKY RAILWAYS

George Stephenson invented the train in just the same way that James Watt invented the steam engine – that is, he didn't. But they both deserve to be dead famous for taking a good idea and actually getting it to work. George himself was partly responsible for the idea that he invented trains – he liked to give the impression that his successes were all his own and that he didn't rely on anyone else.

George Stephenson, cow preserver

George was born in 1781, when James Watt was 45. He was in a great position to be a train inventor because his dad looked after a steam engine. And, like Watt but unlike Leonardo, he was born at exactly the right time for his inventions to catch on. George got a job when he was about nine, keeping an eye on some cows so they didn't wander on to the local railway and get run over by the horse-drawn trains. George was a bright lad and after being given a fascinating new job sorting coal into different sizes, he became an expert on steam engines, working as an assistant to his dad until, when he was 17, he got another job – as his dad's boss!

Until then, George had had no time for any education, but he realized he could really do with some, so he went to night-school when he was 18. (Though he never really got into reading, writing or arithmetic.) It was rare in those days for someone without much money or education to get very far in life. Maybe that's why George had a bit of a chip on his shoulder and was so scathing about scientists who came up with theories but didn't like getting their hands dirty. George also married and had a son called Robert, who was going to be nearly as famous as he was. George loved Robert, but he made him work very hard, both at books and practical jobs.

The most original thing George invented was actually nothing to do with trains at all – it was a miner's safety lamp, guaranteed not to set off explosions in mines, even when the mine was full of inflammable gas (as they tended to be). Mines were sometimes so dangerously gassy that, instead of lamps, miners used to work by the glow from rotting fish skins they stuck to themselves (an ideal experiment to try yourself, by the way). Sometimes firemen were

recruited to help. Not to put out burning mines though! In the 18th century, firemen were people who were sent down gassy mines with candles on sticks. The sticks were fairly long, and the firemen were given wet sacks to wear to protect them from flames if there *was* an explosion, but still it was probably about as much fun as working with The Miner's Friend.

George's wasn't the first type of safety lamp – that had been invented in 1813 by a Dr Clanny, but it was huge and clonky and needed constant messing about with. (Mind you, George never claimed his *was* first – though he wasn't keen to give other people too much credit, he never exaggerated his own discoveries.) George's invention was much simpler, but sadly something very similar was invented at about the same time by Sir Humphry Davy.

The only real difference was that Humphry's had no glass chimney. This made George's lamp a lot safer: Humphry's could get red-hot and cause explosions, while George's just went out if there was much gas about, as he checked himself by taking one down a gas-filled mine.

When it got a bit dangerous, George went on alone, calmly noting the changing colour of the lamp as it got itself ready to go out – or, of course, explode! He was quite sure he was right (as he always was) and that it *would* just go out, but it must have been a somewhat scary experiment even so.

In what was supposed to be a safer version of this investigation, he and Robert collected gas in bladders, took them home and experimented with them – at which point:

Humphry Davy was furious at the suggestion that someone as uneducated as George might have invented the lamp, and made a bit of a fool of himself by writing angry letters to everyone. George himself didn't get drawn into the debate except to give a short talk explaining how he invented the lamp. This talk scared him a lot more than going down an explosive mine, and he blushed so much that he said he could have 'lit a can[d]le at me face'.

LUCKY THAT DIDN'T HAPPEN DOWN THE MINE THEN!

In inventing the safety lamp, George relied on trial and error – he was totally unlike Archimedes in that he didn't work out theories on paper (or his skin) first. But he was a brilliant practical inventor.

Another of George's early inventions was a baby's cradle automatically rocked by smoke from a chimney stack. No one knows how it worked, but apparently it did.

Bangs and crashes

Though James Watt was convinced that a steam engine couldn't be made to move itself along, lots of other people wanted to have a go. James's engines were far too heavy for the job, so it would be no good just putting wheels on one and expecting it to take you to the shops, because it would only sit there sulking and hissing. At the time, all that was available to drag things about or drive anywhere was...

Now horses are nice, even if they can be a bit snappy and make a lot of...

But they're not ideal. They're not all that strong, they need rest, they need feeding and looking after even when they're not driving, and they're not very fast.

The first steam-powered vehicle was invented when James Watt was 33 and George was minus twelve, but it didn't go on rails. It was designed in 1769 by Captain Nicolas Cugnot and was a wagon with a huge kettle in front, with a built-in coal fire to heat it up. The steam it made was diverted to a pair of cylinders which were connected to the front wheel. But it didn't work too well, and crashed into a house, at the enormous speed of about five kilometres an hour.

Much the same thing happened 32 years later when Richard Trevithick – we met him in the last chapter – built a steam car, which immediately ran off the road and crashed into another house. Trevithick didn't mind though. He was a big, muscly, fun-loving bloke who enjoyed nothing so much as throwing sledgehammers over the roofs of buildings to show how strong he was. After the crash, what did he do? Panic? Not exactly. An eye-witness report said:

> *The Parties adjourned to the Hotel and comforted their Hearts with Roast Goose and proper drinks when, forgetful of the Engine, its Water boiled away, the Iron became red hot and nothing that was combustible remained either of the engine or the house.*

It was obvious that getting steam cars not to crash into houses wasn't going to be easy, so Trevithick tried putting one on rails to make a locomotive. Luckily he didn't have to invent rails specially, because they'd been lying around for ages, since at least the early sixteenth century. They were all made of wood until the 1770s when cast-iron ones were invented. Instead of locomotives, the wagons were pulled by:

GUESS WHO?

In 1804 Trevithick tried his idea out, and built a locomotive that could travel at eight kilometres per hour, and by 1808 he had one that went on rails called *Catch Me Who Can*. It just went round a circular track a few dozen metres across, so it was no good for going on holiday, but people liked riding on it anyway.

Trevithick had lots of problems with his engines. To make them powerful enough to pull themselves along they had to use high-pressure steam, which made them go BANG a lot. In any case, they were generally unreliable, and they were so heavy they broke the rails. So they were fun (in a scary, deadly kind of way) but not much use.

Nevertheless, high-pressure steam was a brilliant step forward and if Trevithick had kept working on it, he might be dead famous today. But he was always off trying new things like steam-powered weapons. In 1811 he set off to make money in South America, which meant that the top steam-engine inventor around was George.

Terror trains
George's big break came in about 1812, when he heard that a steam engine which pumped water from a nearby mine was a bit ... well, pants. He had a quick look at it and then, with enormous self-confidence, he told the operators that he could mend it. He took it apart, modified it, put it together, and doubled the steam pressure. Doubling steam pressure sounded like a brilliant way to cause a massive explosion, so lots of people turned up to watch what would happen when the engine was switched on. What happened was that it went wild, shaking the whole engine house. Everyone got a bit panicky – except for George. And he was quite right.

The engine calmed down, and worked – brilliantly. Big success! All the people who'd turned up to jeer skulked off and George was offered a nice job looking after steam engines at the colliery, at a massive salary of £100. Now he could afford to send Robert to school.

In those days, an exciting new development was that stationary steam engines were used to pull wagons on wooden rails up hills – giving the horses a break.

George and Robert worked together to develop some of these.

By this time, people were getting very keen on the idea of replacing horses as much as possible – they were in short supply because so many were being used by armies fighting the Napoleonic Wars, and their food was pricey now, too.

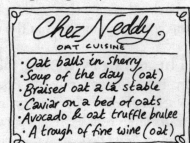

73

So various experimental locomotives were built, but they all had the same problems:

George was determined to solve these problems and make a locomotive that would actually work. Compared to other dead-famous inventors, he didn't make any huge breakthroughs, but he steadily improved the design of steam engines, and was soon building ones that were better than anyone else's. One thing that was special about George is that he paid serious attention to rails as well as what would go on them. In fact, he patented his own cast-iron ones, and ended up with an improved type of wheel/rail system that made trains run more smoothly. It was comfy and meant that the rails didn't break as much.

The mystery of the Blü train

In 1814 George ran his first steam locomotive, the Blücher. This is a bit of a mystery train – no proper plans or drawings of it exist. It's supposed to have weighed 30 tonnes, travelled at six kilometres an hour and had specially shaped wheels so it wouldn't slide sideways off the rails. Anyway, whatever it was, it worked OK, and didn't crash into a single house. It was ever so noisy and did sometimes stop and refuse to start again until someone pushed it, but on the whole it was a success.

So George had built a working locomotive. The only trouble was, nobody had invented anywhere much to go yet; most railways just carried coal or other mine products from the mine to the nearest port or canal.

What was needed now was a bit of a railway network with some stations and ticket inspectors and those trolleys with coffee and sandwiches. Enter Edward Pease. He was a businessman, who wanted to connect Stockton to Darlington with a 25-mile railway. He assumed it would just carry goods, and be horse-drawn. But he appointed George as his chief engineer, and George had other ideas.

Edward raised funds for the project, including £10,000 out of his own pocket, but there were lots of people doing very nicely without locomotives thank you, like the ones who owned canals[1], stage-coaches and horse-drawn wagons. They didn't want to lose their business, and were very resistant to Edward and George's idea. It took lots of argument, and an Act of Parliament, to get the Stockton to Darlington railway off the ground. Or even on it. In fact it needed *two* Acts of Parliament – one for the rails and one for the train. Experts were unhappy about the idea too: even the project's original surveyor had said 'an engine on a public railroad would be a perpetual nuisance'. In fact sometimes it must have seemed to George that everyone was against trains…

1. Canals were *the* way to transport goods before George came along.

So it wasn't easy for George, and he would probably never have succeeded if he'd had any doubt in his abilities. Which he didn't. But though he was the best there was, he wasn't always right…

In 1821 John Birkinshaw developed a new method of rolling wrought-iron rails which made them more flexible. George went to see them and decided they were better than the ones he'd invented and insisted they should be used on the Stockton to Darlington railway, even though it meant he lost a lot of money by not using his own. Edward was soon won over to the new rails, and he managed to talk the other people who were funding the Stockton to Darlington line into agreeing to them too.

When all the rails were down, George and Robert built two nice new locomotives called Locomotion and Hope to go on them, plus a passenger coach called Experiment. The Stockton to Darlington line opened in

1825, the first public railway to use steam locomotives. Even then, some people still thought Locomotion might be an animal – or perhaps 'an automatical semblance of a horse' as someone put it. Everyone who travelled on the line loved it, but not everyone wanted to go to Stockton. Or even Darlington.

George Stephenson, cow menace

So George's next project was a Liverpool to Manchester line. If George had thought the Stockton to Darlington one was tricky, this one seemed impossible – there was even more resistance. Despite the fact that the Stockton to Darlington line was going fine without scaring anyone silly or suffocating them, people still said the new line would 'stop cows grazing, cause hens to cease laying and country inns to close, pollute the air and extinguish horses as a species'. In fact there was so much trouble that the survey had to be done secretly at night.

THE BRITISH BULLDOG

1829

STOP THESE LOCOMOTIVES BEFORE THEY KILL US ALL

The madman Stephenson is at it again. He wants *another* railway line with his lunatic locomotives on it, to connect Liverpool to Manchester this time. But the people of Britain can stop it. Stephenson needs to get Parliament to approve the line. It's up to us to make a stand. Saddle up your horse! Ride to your MP! Let's stop these death-traps in their tracks!

Due to all the shouting, it wasn't easy to get Parliament to allow the line to go ahead. The discussions started off quite well for the railway company. When George was asked whether a cow straying on to the line in the way of a train going at 10 mph wouldn't be 'a very awkward circumstance' he replied, 'Very awkward: for the cow.'

But before long it all started to go a bit wrong. First George let slip that the trains could go at the scary speed of 12 mph. (His advisor stopped him from saying '20 mph', because he would be 'regarded as a maniac'.) Then it turned out that the plans of the route that George had made contained several errors and rough figures (sadly Robert was away when the plans were done, otherwise they'd have been a lot better). In the end, the line was rejected. Which was very annoying. The company had to go through it all again, with a new survey. Even though it passed OK this time, everyone was a bit annoyed with George, what with his wildly exaggerated train speeds and everything, and he was demoted from chief engineer to operative engineer.

Despite the bad start, everyone forgave George when the actual laying of the railway got going. One of his most amazing successes was to lay rails across a 'bottomless' marsh called Chat Moss. Which was a bit – well – *marshy*.

The local papers, liking a bit of excitement, reported this as:

Battle of the trains

While all this was going on, Robert had been working as an engineer in South America: he probably went there because George's dominant nature meant Robert could only really prove himself if he was on his own. But in 1827 he returned and he and George built their most famous locomotive:

George's Secret Notebook

Well, me and the boy've come oop with a right clever loco this time and no mistake. Her's called the Rocket. They'll be a bit of a do when t'committee see 'er, or me name's not George. (Which it is, like.) Take these 'eating tubes: they send the 'eat straight from the coals in the fire-box to the water in the boiler - so there's slathers of 'ot 'igh-pressure steam to make the loco go like a ferret down a rabbit-'ole. Not to mention me special slantin' cylinders, me amazin'ly simple way of linking 'em to wheels, and the spot-on machinin' of the parts. By 'eck, it's a ruddy miracle and no mistake.

The Rocket

Arty bit

Rod to stop Chimney falling over

Chimney into which heating tubes emerge

Piston rod

Boiler, through which 25 heating tubes direct heat from fire box

Nifty new guide rods to stop piston rod vibrating

Controls

Connecting rod

Iron fire box

Man to shovel coal from tender to firebox

Passenger

Water to be turned into steam

Tender Containing Coal

Footplate

81

But there were still plenty of arguments left to have: although the railway was going ahead, it wouldn't necessarily be locomotives that would run on it, and a committee visited the Darlington works to decide. Edward had instructed the engineers to 'have the engines and men as neat and clean as can' but even really scrubbed blokes did no good, and the committee recommended using stationary steam engines to drag the trains about, as had been done elsewhere. George was very cross, but he pulled himself together and wrote a brilliant report to show locomotives were best, and finally they were accepted. Phew.

But ... even then, there was no certainty that the locomotives used on the railway would be George's. Several other people had built their own ones by then and to decide which was best a competition was organized – it was called the Rainhill Trials and it happened in October 1829. There was The Rocket and four other entries...

1. THE NOVELTY – THIS WENT QUITE FAST, BUT BLEW UP. ONCE IT HAD BEEN REPAIRED, IT SPRAYED EVERYONE WITH WATER. IT WAS REPAIRED AGAIN BUT ALL ITS JOINTS GAVE WAY.

2. THE SANS PAREIL—THIS WAS HEAVIER THAN THE RULES HAD STATED, BUT IT WAS ALLOWED TO RUN ANYWAY. IT SHOT RED-HOT COKE FROM ITS CHIMNEY, BEFORE VANISHING IN A CLOUD OF STEAM. AFTER WHICH IT WAS A BIT TIRED AND HAD TO BE PUSHED TO THE END OF THE 〰〰 TRACK.

3. THE CYCLOPED—WHICH WAS ACTUALLY A HORSE ON A TREADMILL.

CALL THIS PROGRESS?

4. THE PERSEVERANCE—THIS BROKE THE WAGON THAT WAS CARRYING IT TO THE TRIALS, AND IT ONLY MADE IT THERE ON THE LAST DAY. THE OWNER, HAVING SEEN WHAT THE OTHER CONTESTANTS COULD DO, RECKONED HE HAD NO CHANCE AND WITHDREW, SHOWING NO PERSEVERANCE WHATSOEVER.

I QUIT

The Rocket won the trials easily. The railway was approved, locomotives were going to be used on it and they were going to be George's. So was that it? No. The Stockton to Darlington railway only had one train, but the Liverpool to Manchester line had lots, so before it could be opened George had to design a railway *system* – signals, coupling/uncoupling systems, timetables and everything.
 Finally…

SEPTEMBER 1830 - LIVERPOOL TO MANCHESTER RAILWAY OPENS TODAY

GEORGE DROVE THE 'NORTHUMBRIAN' WITH THE PRIME MINISTER AND TRAIN-LOVING MP WILLIAM HUSKISSON ON BOARD.

THIS IS SO EXCITING!

HE STOPPED THE TRAIN AND SAID…

NOW YOU FOLKS STAY PUT AND WATCH THEM TRAINS GOIN' PAST

BUT… I'LL JUST HAVE A LITTLE WALK ABOUT…

Despite William Huskisson's unfortunate end, 1830 was the year in which the public really accepted railways with locomotives on them, and finally believed it was possible to travel at 12 miles an hour without your head falling off. Suddenly, everyone wanted George to build them a railway, and he was happy to oblige: he travelled 32,000 kilometres between 1835 and 1837 to do it...

On one of his projects, George built an amazing bridge over the Tyne: 1,300 m long, 170 m wide, and 45 m high. Robert got more and more involved in the new railways, and was the engineer for the Birmingham to London line, which met even *more* resistance, if possible, than George's railways had. (An MP called Colonel Sibthorpe even said he 'would rather meet a highwayman, or see a burglar on his premises, than an engineer'.)

85

A world of steam

When, in 1838, George finally retired to a massive mansion, he did actually stop building railways. But he didn't quite stop inventing: one of his triumphs was the straight cucumber. He also liked to draw blood from his guests... He'd then examine it under a microscope and work out everyone's personalities from their blood groups (which had just been discovered). He also sang and wrestled and, while waiting for trains, liked nothing better than showing drivers how to drive and labourers how to dig, just in case they didn't know. And he spent plenty of time complaining about how new advances in steam technology were a waste of time – like the use of higher pressure steam.

Now George had loads of money, he often gave people presents, especially those who'd helped him in the past. He used to send crates of fruit to his friends, but he

always insisted the cheap wooden boxes he sent them in were returned to him first-class – by rail of course.

Thanks to James and George, the steam age had now really arrived, and people were fascinated by steam power. All sorts of weird inventions emerged, including steam washing machines, a *walking* steam vehicle, a steam-powered walking-and-cigar-smoking metal man that Leonardo would have loved, and even some steam-powered flying machines (but they didn't work too well and you'll have to wait for a few more chapters for a proper one). A lot more railways were laid too: there are now over two million kilometres of railway, enough to rail the Moon's orbit with.

George wasn't too keen on all this – he reckoned any new inventions were rubbish and that only his engines were any good, but most other people were very impressed, and a lot of them changed their minds completely...

George was probably the greatest-ever railway engineer: both his rails and his locomotives were the best there were, and the railway revolution was largely his doing. Which means George was a big factor in making the Victorian period the way it was: full of prosperity, progress, technology, speed and steam. And yet, though George was brilliant, domineering, full of confidence and optimism, without Robert's superior engineering training and administrative skills, it's doubtful whether he would have got very far.

Railways quickly spread over the USA as well as Britain, where they provided a job *and* a workshop-on-wheels to the most famous inventor of all, whom we're about to meet.

GEORGE STEPHENSON
THAT WAS YOUR LIFE

TOP INVENTIONS:
- first locomotive that really worked
- first railway that really worked
- miners' safety lamp

ALSO DEAD FAMOUS FOR:
being about the greatest engineer ever

THOMAS EDISON AND HIS INNUMERABLE INVENTIONS

Thomas Alva Edison slept standing up, made the first *Frankenstein*, and invented a spaceship that he flew to Mars to wipe out the Martians. And, as well as more than a thousand other things, he invented the light bulb.

Honest. All except for that bit about the light bulb.

Tom was born in Ohio, USA in 1847. The United States in those days was an amazing place, full of new ideas, a rapidly spreading population, lots of money and an awful lot of gas lamps. The gas lamps were OK – much better than stumbling about in the dark – but they had their problems: in particular, they were a bit on the dim side. Much like Tom himself, if you listened to his teachers.

HE'S ADDLED, THAT'S WHAT HE IS!

HE'LL NEVER AMOUNT TO ANYTHING, THAT BOY!

HOPELESS!

But Tom's mum knew better. She stopped him from going to school…

And taught him herself instead…

She encouraged him to read all sorts of books – fiction as well as non-fiction. (His dad gave him ten cents for each one he read.) But however clever Mrs E was, she couldn't have known how clever Tom was going to be. He was good at almost everything, except spelling. He might have turned out to be good at maths, but he had a go at reading Isaac Newton's *Mathematical Principles of Physics*, which put him off maths for life. (It *is* a bit terrifying.)

Jobs and journeys

When he was 12, Tom reckoned it was time to go out and earn a living. (I know. Scary idea, but the 19th century was like that.) He got a job on the railway, selling sweets and newspapers. Tom was ambitious, and after a while he started to write and print his own newspapers, using part of the train as his office. When the American Civil War came along in 1861, he got station-masters to chalk up headlines in their stations – he paid them with free copies of papers. This meant people were extra-interested in what was going on, and keen to buy his papers – even when he put the prices up. Clever, eh? Especially considering marketing was in its infancy then…

Tom also included jokes in his paper: '"Let me collect myself," said the man when he was blown up by a powder mill' may not be funny now, but in the 19th century … it probably wasn't funny either.

When he was about 13, Tom started to go deaf, maybe as a result of catching scarlet fever. He reckoned this was actually a good thing, because he wasn't so easily distracted.

Later on, when he was dead famous (and dead rich), Tom also said being deaf saved him from being swindled because he insisted people write down any dodgy deals instead of just talking him into them.

Tom especially liked chemistry and had a laboratory in his parents' basement, with all the bottles carefully labelled 'Poison', just to be on the safe side. But for some inexplicable reason, his mum wasn't too happy with this, and Tom transferred a lot of his favourite chemicals to the train. Where, sadly, they caught fire and burnt up a lot of train before anyone could stop them. Tom did have a tendency to set things on fire a bit. Once it was a whole barnful of hay and another time, when his whole laboratory was burning down, he phoned all his friends to tell them to come and watch.

Perhaps it wasn't entirely unconnected with the fire that the train company sacked him.

However, soon after, he rescued a little boy from certain death when he snatched him out of the way of an oncoming train, much like a scene in one of those silent films Tom hadn't invented yet. The boy's father had no money, but he rewarded Tom by teaching him Morse code and showing him how to use the telegraph. This was just what Tom wanted – telegraphs then were as exciting and new as e-mail was a few years ago.

Anyway, Tom became a brilliant telegraph operator. To use the telegraph, people would write messages which Tom would translate into Morse code. He'd then tap out the code, sending it down a wire to a telegraph operator in another town, who would translate it back to the original message. It was easy for Tom to get a job because lots of operators were off fighting in the Civil War (Tom was too young).

When the war ended, Tom decided it was time to leave home and explore America. After all, he *was* fourteen. He became a 'tramp operator', working in telegraph offices all over the country, and also developing his first invention, a machine which would automatically repeat a piece of code sent to it.

But after a while the jobs ran out and he returned home with no money – to find his parents had none either, because his father had lost his job. So Tom really did have to grow up then. He got a job 1,500 kilometres away in Boston, again as a telegraph operator, at the Western Union Company.

Boston was an amazing place, full of new technical developments, new businesses, and people interested in new technology like telegraphs. While Tom was in Boston, he invented a clever machine which could automatically register people's votes. He thought it would be a great improvement on the existing system, in which a politician would propose something and the audience would fill in bits of paper to say whether they agreed. Each vote had to be manually recorded, so the whole thing took over an hour. Tom patented his invention to make sure no one nicked the idea, but he needn't have worried – even though it would have worked perfectly, the politicians hated it. They didn't WANT to hurry things up.

While a vote was being counted, they could see how it was going, and had a chance to talk people into changing their minds, make deals with other politicians or leave the country. What's the point of being a politician if you can't do things like that?

After a year, Tom was sacked from Western Union for not concentrating on his work, and he moved on to New York, where he couldn't find a job and nearly starved to death. But then something amazing happened. Business people relied on an invention called a stock-ticker, which tapped out messages on a long strip of paper. The messages were about stocks and shares and things, and when a stock-ticker broke down...

Tom was really getting into inventing things now. He plucked up courage to sell a whole lot of improvements to stock-tickers to Western Union for $3,000, but he didn't quite dare ask for so much money, and suggested that Marshall Lefferts, the agent, should make him an offer. Marshall offered him $40,000. It was the only time in Tom's life that he felt like fainting. But he pulled himself together and became the most famous inventor in the world instead.

Inventorissimo

Tom was always a bit scathing of people who thought he just dreamed up his inventions. He had a highly practical and organized mind and could visualize complex problems and solve them logically: and now he had the money to try. He sent plenty of cash to his parents, and used the rest to open a manufacturing shop, where he made stock-tickers. From then on, he invented like mad, starting off by sorting out the multiple telegraph, an idea which Alexander Graham Bell turned into a telephone, as we'll find out when…

AH! YES, NOW THE MULTIPLE TELEGRAPH WAS A MACHINE WHICH COULD SEND SEVERAL SIGNALS DOWN THE SAME CABLE AT ONCE. I SOON REALIZED…

…as we *will* find out *when* we get to the next chapter.

Soon Tom was making so much money with his inventions that he moved into a proper laboratory at Menlo Park, New Jersey, where he employed several assistants. He was bit of a workaholic – he often worked for 20 hours a day and he expected his employees to do the same. Once he worked for 72 hours without sleep, and sometimes he'd fall asleep standing up. Luckily, most of his assistants were ever so keen, just like he was.

Tom was married by then, with three children. Tom nick-named the first two Dot and Dash (which is what telegraph operators called the short and long signals they used). But he didn't see much of his family. He had all that inventing to do…

ZZZZZZZ

IT'S GOOD OF DADDY TO PLAY COWBOYS AND INDIANS WITH US!

In 1876, Alexander Graham Bell invented the telephone. But it wasn't brilliant, because the signal was too weak to travel for long distances. The trouble was that the thing that converted the sound waves into electrical signals was a bit feeble. Tom came up with a much better device called a carbon button. In this, a thin sheet of metal was allowed to just touch a piece of carbon. An electric current did its best to flow between the sheet and the button. When a person spoke into it, the sound waves pressed the sheet firmly on to the button, so the current could flow strongly. In that way, the current that flowed varied with the pressure of the sound waves; so the pattern of current mimicked the pattern of sound, and Tom had a way of making a nice strong signal, which could travel for hundreds of kilometres.

So Tom came up with a brilliant invention of his own. He'd discovered previously that a piece of acid-soaked chalk would slide easily across a piece of metal if there was an electric current present (just the sort of thing anyone might happen to spot – you've probably noticed it yourself). So in his clever telephone receiver, a rotating piece of chalk dragged at a piece of metal to a greater or lesser extent depending on the strength of the electrical signal. The changing drag of the chalk made the metal sheet vibrate in time with the changing strength of the signal. So an electrical signal generated by sound waves at one end of a telephone line could be converted to vibrations in a metal sheet at the other end – and those vibrations formed sound waves again. The only thing was – how to make the piece of chalk rotate?

In 1877, Tom invented one of his most famous gadgets – the phonograph, the ancestor of the record player. (Your most ancient relatives might just be able to remember record players – the ones who say 'Of course, pop music was a lot better in the '70s.')

The phonograph was a little bit like the telephone, except that, instead of generating an electrical signal, sounds were used to make a needle vibrate and make scratches on a sheet of tinfoil wrapped around a rotating cylinder.

When the tinfoil was rotated again, the scratches moved the needle about and its vibrations were turned back into sounds, just the same as the original sounds except for being very quiet and scratchy and tinny.

One reporter said that when he listened to a recording of a violin performance, all he could make out was whether or not the violin was playing. But people had never heard anything like it. They paid good money to hear crackly recordings of just about anything.

Top of the POPS, 1880

1. An extremely slushy love-song
2. Someone telling very bad jokes in a very loud voice.
3. Barking dogs
4. Double-bass sonata (played on the tuba so there's something to hear)
5. A very droney speech by a politician

GROOVY!

Now that Tom had started off an invention that was to lead eventually to boy bands, he thought it was about time he invented electric light. Sadly, Joseph Swan, a man with a beard almost as scary as a book by Isaac Newton –

HEY!

– had done this already, but his light bulbs didn't last very long. Neither did Tom's, to start with. In fact, if you switched one on ***NOW, YOU'D PROBABLY ONLY HAVE GOT TO ABOUT HER***e before it went out again.

Edison's excitingly electrifying enterprise

Thomas Edison's Amazing Phonographic Diary
(Patented, so don't get any ideas, y'hear)

Monday, kinda late

I cannot bu-lieve how tricky this damn light-bulb business is. It should be easy: when 'lectricity goes through somethin', the thing heats right up. The more 'lectricity, or the thinner the thing, the hotter it gets. If it gets darn hot, it starts to glow red. To make it glow white, you have to get it a helluva lot hotter. But sure 'nuff, once you get something that hot, the dang thing tends to catch right on fire, which is kinda nice in some ways, but not what I need here.

Tuesday, round sundown

I sucked the air outta the bulb, like Joe Swan, and that stopped the glowing gizmo – this here filament – from busting into flames, but the *CRACKLE* thing just melted right away. I'll just have to find me something to make the filament outta that won't melt.

Wednesday, around fourteen months later
This *CRACKLE CLICK HISS CRACKLE* invention is a real *CRACKLE TAPTAPTAP HISS* thing. I've tried over six thousand things to make a filament with, and not one worked: wood, metal, paper, string, even some of Jim's beard hair, and all of 'em just melt right away.

Thursday
Hot dawg! I've done it: charred paper, that's the answer.

A few weeks later
By jiminy, charred Japanese bamboo is even better'n paper. Just switched on the latest light bulb, and it looks hot-diggity tre-mendous. I sure hope folks wanna buy it.

1. So some people say. It's somewhat tricky to see quite why Tom had to actually watch the bulb himself for 40 hours to see how long it lasted.

And it was.

Everyone went wild. Within a few years, there were streetlights and domestic lights all over the world: starting with New York, where the first ever electricity company started off with 52 customers in 1882. And the electricity supply system opened the way for all sorts of other electrical equipment too – lots of it invented by Tom. And in case you feel a bit sorry for Joseph Swan, his company and Tom's joined forces a bit later on, and were soon making bits and pieces for Guglielmo Marconi. (The way that Tom developed a whole system like this is something George Stephenson was good at too.)

As with most new inventions, people were a bit nervous about light bulbs, so little warning notices were necessary:

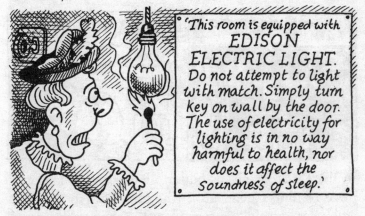

'This room is equipped with EDISON ELECTRIC LIGHT. Do not attempt to light with match. Simply turn key on wall by the door. The use of electricity for lighting is in no way harmful to health, nor does it affect the soundness of sleep.'

Frankenstein, ghosts and Martians

By now, Tom was really, really rich. But that didn't stop him inventing. On the contrary.

The next big thing Tom did was help invent the film industry. As with several of his inventions, all sorts of other people were involved in this too – including the brilliantly named Eadwaerd Muybridge (who had a beard almost as startling as Joseph Swan's). Eadwaerd came to see Tom to show him his moving pictures. Tom loved them, and decided to invent a film camera to make more pictures like Eadwaerd's and a viewer to watch them with. By this time, Tom himself would often just start off an invention and leave his staff to develop it. They tried to build a movie camera, but it wasn't too successful until Tom heard about a new flexible sort of film for use in normal cameras. He got some, cut it into strips, and got his assistant William Dickson to develop a system to pass these strips under a pair of lenses. So Tom and his team built the world's first movie camera, which he called a Kinetograph.

In the Kinetograph, a shutter allows light to fall on a piece of film. Chemicals in the film react to the light and record a single image. Then the shutter closes and the film moves on a step. The shutter opens again and a second image is recorded on a fresh piece of film. And so on.

Like a lot of mechanical inventions, it was a simple idea but incredibly fiddly and annoying to get working.

As Tom put it…

When they'd been developed, the films could be watched through a Kinetoscope – a device in which a light shone through the moving strips into the eyes of the viewer.

One of the first of Tom's films was someone having a really good sneeze – the sort you can really get your teeth into. Encouraged by the success of this, Tom opened the first film studio in the world, and later on his company made the first version of *Frankenstein*. But for a long time, he didn't really think films would catch on.

Tom kept on inventing amazing things for the rest of his life, including:

- a talking doll
- a machine to communicate with the dead (so he said – though no one found any trace of it)
- an underwater telephone
- a way of making plums permanent, lemons last longer and elderberries everlasting.

Like Archimedes and Leonardo, Tom had to help out during wartime (even though – also like them – he wasn't too keen on weapons). In his case, it was the First World War, and he helped develop equipment like periscopes, flame-throwers, and a torpedo-detector.

A lot of Tom's inventions were improved versions of things that existed already – but his improvements often made all the difference between a nice idea and something that was really useful. And he developed things like power stations, refineries and cement factories too – the ideas weren't original, but what was special about them was that they really worked.

Like a lot of people, by the time he was 80 Tom liked a bit of gardening. But he wasn't an ordinary gardener. Rubber was becoming more and more valuable, partly because the car was getting really popular by then, so lots of tyres were needed. But it was expensive to make, so Tom decided to develop a flower that produced rubber. Weird as it sounds, after cross-breeding and examining more than 14,000 plants, he managed it – extracting rubber from a flower called the Goldenrod.

Long before this, Tom had become incredibly famous, even appearing in books like *Edison's Trip to Mars*, by Garrett Serviss. It is a sequel to HG Wells's *The War of the Worlds*, in which Tom invents a spaceship and takes a whole lot of scientific geniuses to Mars to punish the Martians for naughtily conquering the Earth.

When Tom died in 1931, it was suggested that the electricity supply should be switched off all over the world to mark his funeral. But it was soon obvious that this couldn't be done – too many people relied on it by then. Which just goes to show what a great idea it was.

THOMAS ALVA EDISON
THAT WAS YOUR LIFE

TOP INVENTIONS:
- first record player
- improved telephone
- improved light bulb

ALSO DEAD FAMOUS FOR:
inventing hundreds of other things too

ALEXANDER GRAHAM BELL
AND HIS *VERY IRRITATING* PHONE

Alexander Graham Bell invented the telephone, and it made him very rich, very famous, and a little bit bad-tempered. To be honest, he wasn't too keen on it, and thought it was nothing like as useful as the photophone, which was clearly going to be *the* way to communicate in the 20th and 21st centuries.

Aleck, as he was called, was born in 1847, a few days after Edison. In some ways the two men were quite similar – both were keen inventors, both worked on the telephone and the phonograph, both became rich and famous. And deafness was a part of both their lives – Tom was a bit deaf himself and Aleck, whose mother was deaf, was keen on helping deaf people. His father was a teacher of the deaf, who was also very interested in the science of speech. He developed a way of writing down sounds and teaching deaf people to say them. It was called Visible Speech, and it made him famous, but not as famous as Aleck.

Aleck is the only inventor in this book whose dad was a scientist (except Archimedes, though his dad probably frowned on inventors). This was a great help to him, but what really started him off was his grandad. In 1858, Aleck went to a horrible school where he had to do loads of Latin and Greek. School was like that in those days, which was not very helpful for becoming a dead famous inventor – in fact every inventor in this book spent a lot more time at school learning about dead languages than science.

When Grandad heard how badly Aleck was doing, he invited him to stay with him in London for a year. Grandad Bell was a speech scientist like Aleck's father, and he introduced fifteen-year-old Aleck to science. Aleck enjoyed his year, but it made him grow up fast: he had no friends of his own age in London, and his grandad encouraged him to think, talk and act as an adult.

After his year away, Aleck's dad came to fetch him, but before they went back to Scotland, they went to visit a scientist called Charles Wheatstone. Charles showed Aleck a machine that spoke!

Actually, it wasn't that scary: more of a box of tricks really, which Wheatstone had built partly to demonstrate how different speech sounds are made, but mostly just for fun.

To use it you simply had to pump the two sets of bellows, flick the levers, squeeze the resonator, and it would say things like 'Swheeeezshhhhhh'. It looked like this:

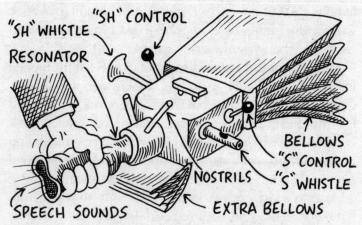

Back in Edinburgh, to encourage Aleck's interest in science and keep him occupied, his dad challenged him and his brother to build a speaking machine themselves. Aleck loved the idea, and wanted to make a whole artificial head, but in the end he made do with rubber lips and cheeks and teeth made of a plastic-like material, cast from a human skull.

Except for a quite clever device to remove the husks from wheat, this was Aleck's first invention, even if it was mostly a copy of another one.

The machine wasn't the sort of thing you'd want to chat to – apart from looking a bit scary, it didn't really speak. It did make a noise like a baby though – a baby with something wrong with it apparently, because a neighbour came round to see what was the matter.

Now that Aleck was suddenly all grown up, he applied for a job – as a teacher on the north coast of Scotland. His brother Melly did too. They didn't tell their dad – but they put him down as a reference, so he soon found out when Principal Skinner got in touch with him. Aleck's dad was a nice bloke, so he said he *could* be a teacher of music and elocution – but only for a year. Then he had to go to university for a year to learn things. (Meanwhile Melly had to go to university for a year, after which he could teach if he still wanted to).

So, in 1863, Aleck started his teaching job. He was only 16, which meant he was younger than some of his pupils. He liked the job, though he started to have headaches which he would suffer from for the rest of his life. His mum told him they were due to pickles, so he stopped eating them, but it didn't seem to help that much. Being a scientific sort of person, he also experimented with speech – by tapping his throat while doing weird things with his mouth in the mirror at night to investigate vowel-sounds.

AAH, EEEEH, I, OWE, OOOOH!

His room-mate thought this was a little odd, but being thought odd doesn't put inventors off a bit (wait until you meet John Logie Baird).

Aleck experimented at home, too…

I'D LOVE TO BE AN INVENTOR AND BUILD A REAL SPEAKING MACHINE. BUT I NEED TO DO SOME EXPERIMENTS FIRST, TO FIND OUT ABOUT SPEECH. BUT EXPERIMENTS ON WHAT? OR… WHO?

Aleck didn't manage to make a machine that could talk properly, but he did get his dog to say 'How are you, Grandmamma?' (ruffly speaking). Everyone was very impressed and amused except possibly the dog, though it never said it wasn't.

A lot of shouting

In 1870, both of Aleck's brothers died. Their parents were sure the climate was partly to blame, and the same year they whisked Aleck – who wasn't too well himself at the time – off to Canada. Whether he'd really have died in Scotland or not, he was certainly soon well again in Ontario. His dad got a job in Canada as a teacher of the deaf, and also visited Boston in the United States, not far to the south of Ontario, where there was a school for the deaf. The head teacher there asked him if he'd come and teach his visible speech, but he was too busy and sent Aleck instead. Aleck loved the work, and was very successful. In fact, he was so good he started his own speech school the next year, and the year after he was made a Professor of Vocal Physiology at Boston University – aged only 26. Teaching kept Aleck busy, but he had time for some top-secret inventing too.

It's not surprising that Aleck should be keen on inventing, nor that he should keep his inventions secret and locked away so no one could pinch the ideas: the world was getting all modern and wanted new inventions and Boston was stuffed silly with inventors in those days, including Tom Edison.

Aleck's Lost Lab Book

There seem to be inventors everywhere, all working on telegraphs. Which isn't very surprising since telegraphs are really popular. Everyone wants to use them. Trouble is, only one message can be sent down a cable at once, so if there's just one cable connecting two towns, only one message can be sent at a time. The only answers are to lay lots and lots of expensive cables

£ 26342·10
£ 2699·29
£ 9277·00
£88266·32
£431814/34·74

very expensive

PTO→

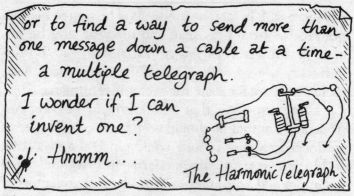

or to find a way to send more than one message down a cable at a time – a multiple telegraph.

I wonder if I can invent one?

Hmmm...

The Harmonic Telegraph

The Harmonic Telegraph, and the phone idea it led Aleck to, is based on the idea of harmonic vibrations, or resonance. Dame Nelly Melba, an opera singer who turns up in the next-but-one chapter, was supposed to be able to break wine glasses by singing at them at exactly the right pitch (very loudly). If you bang the right key on a piano, a guitar-string across the room will sound. If you turn

your telly up loud, you'll probably hear bits of it vibrate. All this is because objects have particular natural ('resonant') frequencies at which they will vibrate strongly ('resonate'). Aleck was investigating how to make a set of tuning forks resonate by using electrical vibrations in wires rather than sound vibrations in the air. The idea was that he could send several signals at once, all at different frequencies – then each tuning fork would respond only to the signal sent at its resonant frequency.

114

It was a good idea, but sadly Aleck wasn't a brilliant technician, and the work was very fiddly so he didn't make much progress. After a while he swapped the forks for steel strips, but it still didn't work.

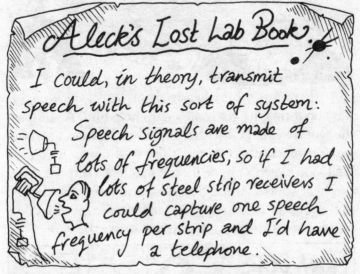

Aleck's Lost Lab Book.

I could, in theory, transmit speech with this sort of system: Speech signals are made of lots of frequencies, so if I had lots of steel strip receivers I could capture one speech frequency per strip and I'd have a telephone.

Actually, as we'll soon see, he didn't need anything as complicated as this, and anyway he never built it because he thought any electrical signal the transmitter could generate would be so weak that the receiver would never pick it up, so it wasn't worth trying.

Aleck had a girlfriend called Mabel, who had been one of his pupils. One evening he went round to her dad's house. Dad was Gardiner Hubbard, one of the wealthiest businessmen in Boston. Aleck entertained him by singing loudly into a piano and making different strings resonate. He explained that electrical signals could do the same thing. Being a businessman, Dad said 'So what?' Aleck told him it could be the secret of a multiple telegraph that could cope with more signals than Tom's version. Excitedly, Gardiner offered to back Aleck's research.

Now there was a bit of cash about, Aleck reckoned it was about time he got someone to help him. Apart from the fact he could do with a skilled technician, it would make it much easier to test things – I mean, if you say 'helloooo' down a phone it's not much of a surprise if you can hear yourself is it?[1] So it's hard to tell if your phone is working. What you need is someone else several rooms away to see if they can hear you through the wire.

So Aleck found an assistant called Watson and they set up a laboratory and got to work on the harmonic telegraph (and a terrifying machine we'll get to later). And then, in 1875, Aleck accidentally invented half a telephone...

1. Actually, when phones got going and people annoyingly rang Aleck up, he used to say 'Hoy hoy' instead of 'Hello'.

Aleck was still experimenting with his steel strips, each of which only vibrated strongly at its resonant frequency. He and Watson sent electrical signals down the wire to make the strips resonate, but the strips would often get jammed and need a good flicking to free them again.

One day in June, when no signals were being sent for the moment, Watson tried to unjam a stuck strip at one end of the wire while Aleck was pottering about at the other. Watson gave the strip a really good twang – and, at Aleck's end of the wire, a strip twanged!

Aleck was amazed, and told Watson to keep twanging. Each time Watson twanged his strip, Aleck's twanged too – yet the electrical transmitter was switched off! Aleck realized that the only explanation was that the moving strip, with the small amount of magnetism still in the transmitter when it was switched off, had made its own tiny electrical signal, to which Aleck's strip had responded. It was just like banging a key on a piano and a guitar-string vibrating in sympathy, but the signal was being sent as electricity, rather than as sound.

But there was more to it than that. When Aleck stuck his ear against the strip, the single pure note changed to a nice broad twang made of a range of frequencies. The fact that it now responded to a *range* of frequencies made it a basic telephone receiver. Aleck was astonished that there was enough power in a flick of Watson's thumb to make an electrical signal strong enough to make another strip vibrate, and that a single strip could respond to so many frequencies at once. He had discovered that it was much simpler to build a phone than anyone had imagined, for three reasons:

1. Strong electrical signals can be made and detected quite easily by vibrating steel strips, given a little magnetism.

2. Even though a steel strip has a preferred frequency at which it likes to vibrate, it will respond happily to a range of frequencies if it is 'damped' by being touched or held gently. So it can respond fairly well to all the frequencies in the human voice.

3. Because speech is a mix of different frequencies, you might think that a telephone has to produce a whole lot of electrical signals, each with a different frequency, and make sure that the different electrical frequencies don't merge together. This sounds very tricky, and a lot of people spent a lot of time coming up with really complicated ways of ensuring the frequencies didn't merge. But they needn't have bothered – the frequencies don't *want* to merge, thanks very much, and don't need keeping apart. It's just like sound waves in the air or vibrations in the string of a toy telephone – the different

frequencies don't need to be kept separate, they do it themselves.

Aleck's earlier phone idea had been quite complicated, with each frequency kept separate from the others by means of a whole series of steel strips, one per frequency. And he'd assumed that the electrical signals produced by the wobbles of a steel strip set in motion by the human voice would be far too weak to make another strip wobble. But he was wrong. (Not that Aleck wasn't brilliant to sort the phone out – a lot of scientific discoveries, like evolution, seem totally obvious once someone else has thought them up.)

DOH! IT'S *50000* OBVIOUS NOW!

SMACK

Aleck didn't have a phone yet – all he had was a receiver. To have a really satisfactory chat, you need to be able to talk as well as listen. But Aleck and Watson were halfway to a transmitter too, since they'd managed to generate an electrical signal from a flicked reed rather than from an electrical power source. If they could develop a way of getting the human voice to move the transmitter reed instead of Watson's thumb, they'd really have managed to invent the telephone. So Aleck started work on a transmitter. It didn't look much like today's ones and it wasn't very handy either – in fact it was a pot full of acid, and it worked like this...

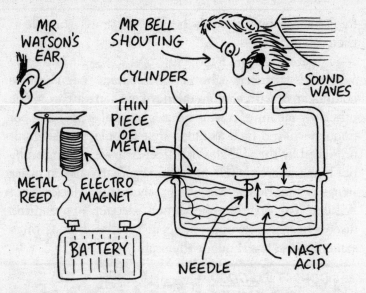

MR WATSON'S EAR

MR BELL SHOUTING

CYLINDER

THIN PIECE OF METAL

SOUND WAVES

METAL REED

ELECTRO MAGNET

BATTERY

NEEDLE

NASTY ACID

The handy thing about acid is that, unlike water, it conducts electricity brilliantly. The more of the metal needle was submerged in the acid, the bigger the area in contact with the acid, and the more electricity flowed. So the strength of the current depended on the amount of the needle which was submerged. When the metal plate vibrated in response to a good loud shout, a section of the needle moved rapidly in and out of the acid. The quickly changing amount of submerged needle generated a quickly changing electrical current – so the acid phone was a way of converting shouts into changing electrical currents.

The currents were used to alter the strength of an electromagnet, which pulled on a metal reed – so as the currents wobbled in time with Aleck's voice, the reed wobbled too, and reproduced the sounds. In an unconvincing kind of way.

How not to be a dead-famous inventor

Although Aleck didn't have a working phone yet, he thought he might manage it one day, so to be on the safe side he patented the idea, on 14 February 1876. He was just in time. A few hours later another inventor, Elisha Gray, turned up at the patent office, also to patent a phone. Though Aleck didn't realize it, he wasn't the only one who wanted to ring people up: in fact, Elisha's phone was very similar to Aleck's, so if he'd been a few hours earlier, he might be dead famous today, instead of Aleck. He'd also have been rich – Aleck's patent was probably the most valuable ever. But Elisha just wasn't convinced the phone would be any use to anyone so he didn't patent it for absolutely ages. Which just goes to show that a successful inventor needs to think his invention is great, even when no one else does.

On 10 March 1876, Aleck said 'Mr Watson, come here, I want to see you' into his acid phone, and, three rooms away, Watson heard him. Watson later said Aleck called him when he'd poured acid on his trousers, but Aleck didn't mention this, and anyway, if you'd done that, wouldn't you be more likely to say...

But that's not the end of the story. Inventors need to be salesmen as well as scientists, and Aleck couldn't rely on the phone selling itself, especially being full of acid. Luckily, he was a bit of a showman when he put his mind to it, and he organized demonstrations of his new invention all over the place. The only thing was, the phone wasn't very reliable, very clear or very loud. So – cunningly – he didn't use it as a telephone when he demonstrated it! Instead he impressed people with tricks like getting a little box to make a sound like an organ, a gimmick only partly based on his phone.

One of Aleck's scarier lectures was to the very famous and very serious American Academy of Arts and Sciences. But he needn't have worried – they liked him and his invention so much they clapped. It was the first time they'd applauded anyone in over twelve years (so they must have had rather dull meetings).

Aleck's Lost Lab Book

12 June 1876

It's all very well demonstrating phones to scientists. but I could do with some real publicity. It's already 1876 and in another century or so

People will be wanting car-phones so I'd better get production of mine going soon. — Just a minute...

Hmomm...1876 - 1 century =

1876 - 100 = ~~1776~~ **1776** ✓

Got it! It's a century this year since the United States was formed. There must be loads of dos and shindigs and suchlike, full of people worth impressing. Surely I can wave my phone about at one of them!

25 June 1876

Had a brilliant day today. Took my phone to a big centennial exhibition and got the Emperor of Brazil to try it out. And he loved it! The Emperor actually ran about shouting 'I hear! I hear! It talks!' REALLY LOUDLY. It's just the publicity I need!

The telephone still needed work as well as publicity, so Bell and Watson worked. Systematically, they varied each part of the telephone to see what would make it better. At one point, Bell thought that the best type of phone might have a speaker made of a plate of steel 6 mm thick and 60 cm square. Luckily for all of us, Aleck reckoned it wouldn't work too well, and dropped it.

The telephone certainly did need improving, though...

THE DAILY SHOUT

1876

DON'T CALL US, MR BELL!

Telephones. What a great idea ... not! An ideal ornamental gift, a source of great fun for the kiddies to try to work out what the person at the other end is saying, and a great way of using up any spare cash. But as a means of communication – I don't think so.

And even if they did work, isn't it all a bit, well, spooky? Disembodied voices travelling down wires and all that. Could our brains cope with receiving messages in such a weird way?

And wouldn't they make us terribly lazy? We'd never get out in the fresh air again!

Mr Bell: Mad scientist

One reporter said a voice over the phone sounded like 'someone a mile away being smothered', or someone with 'his mouth full and his head in a

barrel;' a psychiatrist claimed that phones could drive

people mad, and said that 'excitable persons' should never use them; and some religious people called telephones 'Devices of Satan', because they'd make people lazy.

Later on, Aleck demonstrated telephones in all sorts of ways and places – including underwater…

He also went to England and showed his telephone to Queen Victoria. Fortunately, Aleck had managed to design an acid-free receiver by then, so there were no diplomatic incidents. (There could have been, though – Aleck was used to touching the hands of deaf people to attract their attention, and he touched the Queen's hand without thinking. Touching the Royal Person, as the Queen's body was called, was ever so dodgy, but she managed to cope and didn't scream or throw Aleck in the Tower of London or anything.)

> *Indeed Mr Bell I can assure you I am, if I may be permitted to speak with candour, somewhat impressed by your remarkable... ah ... telephonic apparatus.*

Aleck soon returned to America.

Though Aleck kept improving his phone, it was actually Tom who came up with the invention that really fixed it (see page 97), and eventually his method took over from Aleck's. By then, though, the Bell Company had been formed, with Aleck as a director. The company became one of the richest in the world and, in a later version called AT&T, it eventually operated over 100 million phones (and became a major rival of Guglielmo Marconi and John Logie Baird's companies along the way).

But it wasn't all sitting about eating chocolate for Aleck: over the years 600 people built phones which used Aleck's ideas without his permission, and 600 times the Bell Company (and that usually meant Aleck himself) had to complain about it in mind-shrivelling detail in court. Aleck once spoke for seven hours at one of these hearings. When the lawyers asked him if he'd like to break for lunch, Aleck just said, 'I don't lunch,' and went on with his explanation.

Seeing by ear, hearing by light

The Bell Company was an amazing success, and the value of its shares rose and rose. Aleck had plenty of them, so he was soon very rich indeed, quite rich enough to retire and spend more time helping deaf people, so that's what he did. He'd never been very keen on the business side of the company, especially all the court cases. And he was a bit tired of the phone itself: he'd spent most of his life fiddling about with it, and he didn't want to be known only for inventing it and nothing else.

Retiring didn't mean no more inventing of course – inventors never do stop inventing. As he said:

Wherever you may find the inventor, you may give him wealth or you may take from him all he has; and he will go on inventing. He can no more help inventing than he can help thinking or breathing.

127

Aleck's disembodied ear

Aleck had already invented a few other things, like a handy device you could wave in the air which would shout, 'Help, help!' and spinning tops which swore when you stuck a pencil into them. Surprisingly enough, these two didn't catch on. Aleck also invented something called an ear phonautograph. He made it from iron, a bit of hay, and a dead person's ear. And not just the floppy bit either – there were some innards and plenty of hair and scalp and ear-wax too, covered with oily stuff to keep it nice and squidgy.

Aleck put it together like this…

…and shouted at it. The ear's drum wobbled in response, just like a living one, and the bit of hay wobbled too and formed a pattern on a piece of smoked glass. Aleck had made his shout visible! (Later, Aleck replaced the ear with metal reeds, to everyone's relief.)

Another of Aleck's inventions, which he reckoned was greater than the telephone, was called the photophone. It would allow people to telephone each other without using wires. It worked like this:

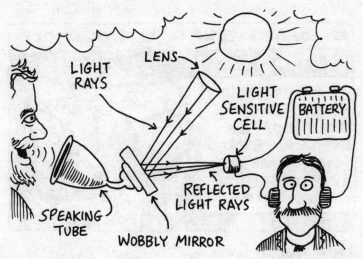

The photophone would only work if you could see whom you were talking to, and if it wasn't raining or misty. Even then, it was limited in range to about 200 m. But it might have caught on, at least in a small way, if it hadn't been for Marconi, whom you'll meet in the chapter after next. One thing it did do was encourage people to investigate television: Bell kept all the details secret for a long time, and people thought he'd invented the telly.

Whatever Aleck hoped, he was dead famous as the inventor of the phone, and people recognized him wherever he went. Even on a train in North Carolina…

How not to fly

In 1881 Aleck got his own back on Tom Edison, by improving one of the other inventor's inventions to such an extent that *his* version took over. Tom had invented the phonograph in 1877, but hadn't done a lot with it since. It was fairly popular, but the problem was that it made its recordings on tinfoil. The foil soon wore out and had to be chucked away – until, in 1881, Aleck developed the wax cylinder instead. This was much better – it lasted longer and gave better sound quality. It became the standard way of recording until flat records were invented in 1887.

Aleck invented other successful things too, including a type of metal detector. He invented this in an attempt to find a bullet in President Garfield, who had been shot by an assassin. Unfortunately, it didn't work, probably because the bullet was too deep, and Garfield died.

(Actually, he didn't die of the bullet but because the doctors didn't wash their hands before they tried to fish it out with their fingers.) However, Aleck's bullet-detecting technique was used successfully on luckier patients.

Not quite all Aleck's inventions were to do with sound. For years he'd been fascinated by flying machines, and in 1891 he became extra keen when he met Samuel Langley, who was obsessed with trying to build one (he turns up in the next chapter). Aleck invented all sorts of experimental flying machines, but they weren't any more successful than Leonardo's, despite the fact that there were now plenty of power sources available.

Aleck tried out lots of them including steam-powered helicopters, spring-powered planes and rockets. He also tried kites. Lots and lots of kites. He became completely obsessed with them, and once built a box kite that was 4.4 m long, 3.2 m wide and 1.6 m high.

Unfortunately, this fascination with kites led Aleck in completely the wrong direction: knowing that kites are easier to fly if they're slow and don't dart about, he decided that ideally planes would be very slow too. The best plane he could imagine would be something like the Starship Enterprise – it would be able to hover motionless in the air, but would never actually land. People would get on and off using little ladders. Sadly this was just not the way things worked out.

However, even if Aleck's planes were pants, his phones were a phenomenon. In 1885 there were nearly 70,000 of them, and 25 years later there were more than a hundred times as many.

THE DAILY SHOUT

1910

THANK YOU, MR BELL!

Telephones! What a great idea! An ideal practical gift, a source of great fun for the kiddies to talk to their friends, and a great way of saving money. And as a means of communication – they're brilliant. Isn't it all amazing – disembodied voices travelling down wires! Could our brains receive messages in a more direct way? And they make us so much more efficient – we'll never have to leave the office to talk to anyone again! Hurrah for telephones and Mr Bell!

Mr Bell : Genius

In 1915, Aleck made another historic phone call – again to Watson. This was on the first transcontinental line, which linked New York to San Francisco. Wittily, Aleck said: 'Watson, come here, I want to see you.' To which Watson, thinking he could be just as amusing, replied: 'But it will take weeks for me to get to you now.'

Aleck would never have a phone in his study. They were just too disturbing. On the whole, he preferred them when they were quiet. But from then on, they never were, except once, in 1922. All the phones in America were silent for one minute to mark his funeral.

ALEXANDER GRAHAM BELL THAT WAS YOUR LIFE

TOP INVENTIONS:
- telephone
- wax cylinder record
- bullet-detector

ALSO DEAD FAMOUS FOR:
spending lots of time and money helping deaf people

THE WRIGHT BROTHERS AND THEIR UNFLAPPABLE FLYING MACHINES

Flying is one of those things which people have always wanted to do. Over the last few centuries, lots of them have had a go, including most of the inventors in this book. It's those little birds that make it so tempting. But they're also the problem. They fly so well, it seemed for a long time that theirs must be the only way: waving your arms about.

OR 'WINGS' AS WE CALL THEM

So, for centuries, people tried to turn themselves into birds – with flapping wings, and sometimes feathers too. It didn't take long for scientists to prove this was impossible – people were just too heavy and weak – but that didn't stop people dressing up as birds and jumping off high buildings, just to check the scientists were right.

134

They always were, of course.

This has always been a problem with inventing things – people are brilliant at copying nature, what's tricky is thinking up something really new, like the mechanical clock, the wheel, or the non-flapping flying machine.

After several centuries, a lot of people were finally convinced that flapping was just for the birds, and had started to try other ways. There are five things that a really satisfactory flying machine must be able to do:

Objective 1 had never been a problem – since AD 1020 or even earlier, a few people had been willing to fling themselves off churches and other high places in the interests of aeronautical research. But they always found Objective 2 a bit tricky: 2.5 seconds didn't really count.

Objective 2 was finally achieved in 1783, by a duck, a cockerel, and … a sheep.

They were the passengers on the first hot-air balloon journey, and were soon followed by people. The idea of a hot-air balloon is simple: when you heat air up, the molecules it's made of move faster, bang into each other harder, bounce off each other more violently and so move further apart. So the hotter a cubic metre of air gets, the fewer molecules it contains and so the lighter it becomes. That's why hot air – from any sort of heater for instance – rises. So all you have to do is put the hot air in a balloon and that will rise too. Which is great fun, so long as you don't set fire to the balloon. Fun, but not very useful because the balloons couldn't really deal with Objective 3. So you never knew quite where you'd end up…

Until 1852, when Henri Giffard used a steam engine to move a balloon about. For a while, airships like this seemed to be the answer – but they could easily catch fire and in any case were enormous, clumsy, slow and couldn't cope with much wind. Flying one was like taking a bouncy castle for a swim. Meanwhile, people were still jumping off things with wings on, but were being slightly more scientific about it, and from the 1840s onwards, several managed to make short glides – or, as in the case of George Cayley, got small children and servants to do it for them.

The most successful of these glider-pilots was Otto Lilienthal, who built a sort of hang-glider in the 1890s. It was his work, and that of George Cayley and Samuel Langley, that helped to inspire Wilbur and Orville Wright, who were born in Indiana in 1867 and 1871.

The Wright stuff

Wilbur and Orville were extra clever, extra industrious, and extra noisy. Luckily, their parents encouraged them (other than noise-wise). Their mum liked making and inventing things, and their dad gave them educational toys, such as a gyroscope – which they took apart, as they took everything apart. (Occasionally they managed to put things back together again.)

Their dad also encouraged them to earn money, and they soon developed into little entrepreneurs like Tom Edison: they hired out goat-drawn wagon rides, and even collected bones so they could sell them to people to make fertilizer out of. They stole some of them from dogs, but they were a bit on the smelly side and the dogs recaptured a lot of them anyway.

Through projects like this, Wilbur and Orville soon learned the value of advertising, even if it was only whingeing to their neighbours. They found a bit of exaggeration didn't come amiss either – when they set up a circus with a friend, they advertised it like this…

To be utterly accurate, the poster should have said:

They sent the advert off to a newspaper with no money to pay for it, but the paper printed it anyway, as a news item, and the circus was highly successful, despite a certain lack of realism when the wolf attacked Red Riding Hood.

The Wrights also made and sold stilts and started a stilt craze in their town. They even used their stilts in a flood to rescue the money of an old lady who'd been driven out of her home by the flood water. A man who claimed to be a policeman tried to get the money off them, but when he refused to show his police badge there was bit of a struggle, from which the real police rescued the Wrights and arrested the man. It was like an Enid Blyton adventure, except they didn't have a dog called Timmy.

The Wrights also liked inventing things (always a handy characteristic in an inventor): when he was a boy, Wilbur invented a machine to fold paper, and, later, they made a new type of rat trap. They also had a go at an automatic-machine-for-taking-your-shoes-off-and-putting-them-back-on-again, but that didn't get beyond the planning stage.

But, like George Stephenson, they were soon focused on one big idea: they wanted to fly. It seemed really easy to start with – if a toy helicopter could fly, why not just make it bigger? It was the same idea Aleck had had about kites – just enlarge them until they're big enough to carry you. But this doesn't work: the Wrights tried enlarging their toy helicopter, and it crashed. Things like that always do, and here's why…

Depressing for Dumbo

Wings help things fly, but weight keeps them on the ground. If a bird has wings 50 cm long and 20 cm wide then the area of each wing will be 50 x 20 = 1,000 cm². Doubling the size of the bird means its wings become 100 cm long and 40 cm wide, so their area increases four times – to 100 x 40 = 4,000 cm². This will give the wings four times their original lifting power.

This sounds very promising, but what happens to the weight of the bird? That depends on its volume, so how does that increase? If the bird's body is 40 cm long, 10 cm wide and 10 cm high its volume is 40 x 10 x 10 = 4,000 cm³. Doubling the size gives 80 x 20 x 20 = 32,000 cm³ – so its volume, and therefore its weight, has increased eight times. So though the lifting power is four times as great, what needs lifting is eight times bigger.

This is why ostriches and elephants can't fly, and you don't get planes as big as a city.[1]

1. The biggest plane ever flown, the Spruce Goose, had a wingspan of 97.5 m and was 66.6 m long. It only ever flew once, in 1947.

This worrying law of nature didn't worry the Wrights at the time, because they didn't know it. Maybe it's just as well – it might have put them off.

Anyone who is going to invent a flying machine needs to be good at engineering, and luckily the Wrights were. They even opened their own bike shop, where they built and repaired bikes as well as selling them. Another thing inventors need to be able to do is publicize themselves, and the Wrights made a good start there too, publishing and printing newspapers for a while. The third thing inventors need is good scientific training – but, like James Watt, George Stephenson and Tom Edison, the Wrights hadn't done too well at school. But two out of three's not bad.

Though the Wrights had been interested in flying since they were children, what really got them going was reading about Otto Lilienthal and Samuel Langley. Wilbur wrote to Samuel in 1897, and he also wrote to the Weather Bureau to find a place suitable for flying. The Bureau said the best place was a place called Kitty Hawk in North Carolina.

Up, up and a...Oops

Otto Lilienthal seemed to have really mastered gliding, until he died in 1899, when his glider crashed because he couldn't manage Objective 4. This Objective was a real problem: people had tried rudders of various sorts but without much success.

The Wright brothers were like James Watt in that there was nothing new about their project, and their machine wasn't the first of its kind, but they managed to invent one key, crucial thing. With James it was the separate condenser. With the Wrights it started with a cardboard box. One day in 1899 Wilbur picked up a long box in the bike shop, 5 cm square by 15 cm long (it had contained an inner tube for a bike tyre). After playing with it for a bit, he found it was easy to twist it without damaging it, once he'd torn the ends off. After a bit more thought, he put together first a twistable bamboo model, then a twistable kite 1.5 m long.

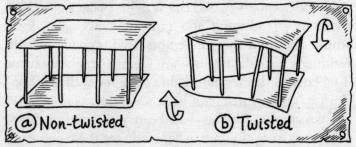

ⓐ Non-twisted   ⓑ Twisted

That was the invention that led the Wrights to solve Objective 4: a biplane with twistable wings should be easy to steer: twisting the back edge of the right wing up and the back edge of the left wing down will mean the right wing falls, the left rises and the plane curves to the right.

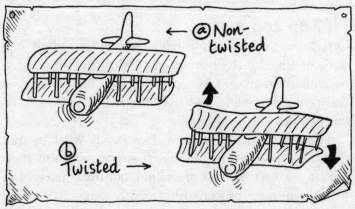

← ⓐ Non-twisted

ⓑ Twisted →

This isn't one of those books that tells you how to make radio-telescopes out of frying-pans and matchsticks, but is does have two little practical experiments. And this is one of them:

- Make a paper aeroplane. It's best to make it fairly wide, so it will fly nice and slowly and you can see what's happening:

- Bend the back edge of the right wing up and the back edge of the left wing down:

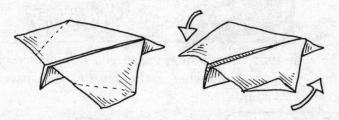

- Throw it gently

And you'll see that...

- The right wing falls, the left wing rises and the plane curves to the right, just as the Wrights hoped it would.
- The plane crashes, just as the Wrights hoped it wouldn't.

The next year, they tested a five-metre long glider at Kitty Hawk, with wings that twisted when they pulled

143

ropes attached to them. It crashed and was smashed to pieces. So what did the Wrights do then? Try a new approach? Give up? No, they rebuilt it and got on board.

Objective 1 was achieved by letting the glider run down a slope (reassuringly called Kill Devil Hill) into the wind, and launch itself off into the air like a ski-jumper (it even had skis). Though it was a bit like flying a wardrobe, it just about worked, and over the next few years the Wrights had many more goes, trying over and over again until they perfected things like where the pilot should be.

Once in 1901, with a new, bigger glider, Wilbur took nine goes to find just where to lie. Finally, he managed to glide 90 metres.

No – but they were now as good as other flyers, like Otto Lilienthal. They could achieve about the same distances. But while their warpable wings and rudders allowed them to keep their gliders on course, they hadn't mastered proper steering – all their flights had been more or less straight lines. And they hadn't had a go at Objective 2 yet – they hadn't tried any powered flights at all. Like Leonardo in the 1480s, it was time to stop tinkering and experimenting and turn themselves into scientists.

First they had to design better wing profiles. It seemed that this wouldn't be too difficult, because Otto had published lots of stuff about 'how to build a perfect wing'. But when the Wrights tried building wings to his recipe, they soon found his data were all wrong – and so were everyone else's. So they had to become even *more* scientific, and built themselves a wind-tunnel in which they could experiment with different wing profiles.

Why did the profiles matter? Because they're what actually lifts the plane, converting some of the forward motion to lift. To understand this, we need a bit of background…

Although we don't notice it, the air is pressing down on us and everything else with a force of about a kilogram every square centimetre. We don't feel this because there's the same pressure inside us, pushing out. It's the same with a balloon: the air outside presses in on it with a force of dozens of kilograms, but the air inside pushes out with an equal force – which is why, if you take your balloon to outer space, where there isn't any air, the force of the air inside will make it pop (and it won't do you much good either, if you don't wear a pressurized suit).

Planes fly because some of the air pressure above the wings is removed, so the pressure below them is greater and pushes them up. And here's experiment number two to prove it:

• Get a strip of paper about 20 cm long and 5 cm wide and hold it at one corner in front of your mouth, like this…

• You might be a bit surprised at what happens if you blow along the top of the strip…

You've just demonstrated the secret of flight:

THE FASTER AIR MOVES ACROSS A SURFACE THE LESS IT PRESSES ON IT

So, planes have wings with profiles like this…

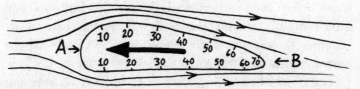

Imagine the wing is moving through the air. Because the top of the wing is longer than the underside of the wing (about 73 cm compared to about 66 cm), the air that flows over it from A to B has further to go than air that flows under it from A to B. So the air that flows above the wing has to go faster than the air that flows under it.

This means that the air above the wing presses down on it less that the air below it: so the wing, and the plane, are pushed up. And the faster the plane flies, the harder it is forced up.

Power planes

During 1902 the Wrights made nearly 1,000 flights in their glider, with its new flashy wing profiles. In the end, sadly…

But never mind, by this time they were fairly happy with all the Objectives except for number 2. It was time to build an engine. At this point, all previous inventors had either given up, stuck to gliding, or tried to use steam engines. But by this time – 1902 – petrol engines were being used experimentally for driving cars and motor bikes. Luckily, the assistant at the bike shop, Charlie Taylor, was a great engineer. He built a light petrol engine to Wilbur's design.

There was one thing they still needed to sort out Objective 2: something to convert the power of the engine to forward motion. A propeller, or even two. Just as with the wing profiles there was design information about – and again it was all wrong. So they spent a long time designing a better one.

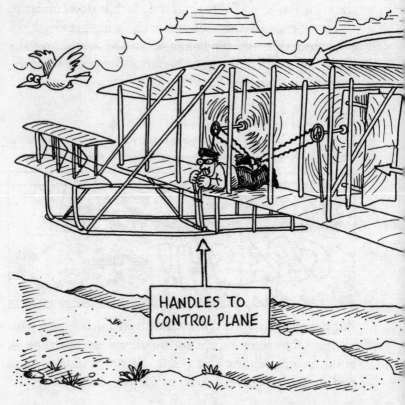

HANDLES TO CONTROL PLANE

Finally, in 1903, everything was ready. Well, actually it wasn't but the Wrights heard that Samuel Langley was doing so well with his own flying experiments that they thought they'd better hurry up and conquer the air now. It wasn't easy – the first thing that happened was that the propellers fell off. But after a lot of trials and tinkering and cursing the Wrights were happy with them. Three days after a failed attempt on 14 December 1903, Wilbur launched himself into the air in a plane hopefully named *Flyer*. It had warpable wings with precise profiles, proper propellers, an energetic engine and a nice pair of skis … and it flew!

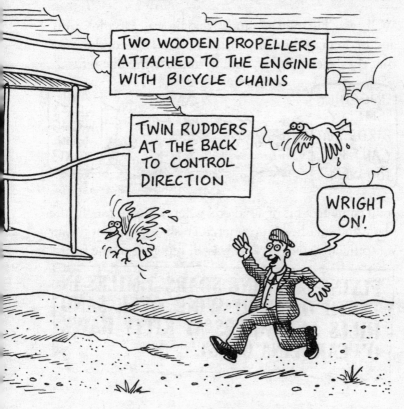

It really did fly: the petrol engine turned the propellers, the propellers screwed their way through the air and pushed the plane forward as Archimedes and Leonardo would have loved, the nicely profiled wings converted some of the forward motion to lift, the wires attached to the wings allowed Wilbur to warp them and control his flight. It was brilliant.

Well, yes, but never mind. Next it was Orville's turn, and he managed to stay in the air for 12 seconds. After that they spent the day taking turns, flying like birds.

It all came to a bit of a sad end when a breeze caught the plane and smashed it up when it crash-landed. But the air was officially *conquered*. It was all reported in the paper:

FLYING MACHINE SOARS 3 MILES IN TEETH OF HIGH WIND OVER SAND HILLS AND WAVES AT KITTY HAWK ON CAROLINA COAST.

Except for the bits about the three miles and the waves it was absolutely correct. The paper also said '"Eureka!" he cried, as did the alchemist of old.' But Wilbur didn't actually say this, just as Archimedes (who wasn't an alchemist) hadn't two thousand years earlier.

From then on, there was no stopping the Wrights: the next year they unveiled *Flyer II*. This was launched in a clever way, by dropping a weight connected to a rope that went over a pulley. It was the first Wright plane to fly in a circle. This flight was reported much more accurately – in the prestigious and highly appropriate journal *Gleanings in Bee Culture*. The editor, Amos Root, had heard about the Wrights and had travelled 280 kilometres to see them fly.

The next year, 1905, the Wrights launched *Flyer III*, which could stay in the air for over half an hour and fly in spirals, circles and figures of eight.

Next the Wrights wrote to the US Secretary of War, offering to sell him a plane. Since he probably didn't read *Gleanings in Bee Culture* and he hadn't known anyone was anywhere near conquering the air, he was probably a little surprised. He turned them down.

So in 1907 the Wrights went to Europe to sell their plane. There, they met an American army officer who got Wilbur a hearing with someone suitably posh and important, and the US Army ordered a Wright plane that could carry two blokes at 40 miles per hour. In 1909 the US Army got its plane, and the same year Wilbur gave a public flying display, with more than a million people watching. Soon after, he flew across the Hudson in New York – and around the Statue of Liberty.

The next year the brothers made their only ever joint flight. Later they took their 82-year-old dad for a spin. He was most impressed, and didn't scream at all.

Though, sadly, Wilbur died of typhoid in 1912, Orville survived to see the planes he'd helped invent go faster than sound.

WILBUR & ORVILLE WRIGHT
THOSE WERE YOUR LIVES

TOP INVENTIONS:
- controllable flight by wing-warping
- first successful powered heavier-than-air flying machine
- scientifically designed propellers and wing profiles

ALSO DEAD FAMOUS FOR:
being American heroes

GUGLIELMO MARCONI
AND HIS ENDLESS ESSES

The soon-to-be-dead-famous inventor checked the electrical connections one last time, took a deep breath and flicked the switch. A spark crackled across the gap between two conductors. Instantly, across the room a tiny copy of the spark flashed – with no connection between them. Radio had been invented. Dramatic, wasn't it?

Nope, it's Heinrich Hertz. He made the first radio transmission in 1887. You couldn't really expect Marconi to do it – he was only 13 at the time.

Well, Hertz's experiment was great, but if there hadn't been any progress from there, you could only send a radio signal to someone in the same room. Cosy, but a bit pointless.

Despite Tom Edison's prediction, what Guglielmo Marconi did for radio was just what James Watt did for steam engines. He took a brilliant idea that wasn't much practical use and made it into something zillions of people could benefit from.

Marconi's magic mum

Guglielmo was born in 1874 in Bologna, Italy. Like James Watt, Tom Edison, Aleck Bell, and the Wrights, he didn't like school or do too well there. But he loved stories about scientists and he was soon inspired to become one himself. He was fascinated by electricity – lots of people were in those days. Guglielmo's favourite scientist was Benjamin Franklin, who had showed that lightning was a type of electricity. Sadly, when

Guglielmo tried copying one of Benjamin's experiments, he broke a lot of the family china. Though his family was rich and could afford plenty more, Guglielmo's dad was NOT happy, and thought Guglielmo's experiments were a complete waste of time, not to mention plates. Luckily, his mum was just the opposite – she thought Guglielmo was great.

Another of the experiments that Guglielmo imitated was more successful – he and a friend set up a metal spike attached to a bell, which rang when there was lightning. He had no idea why it worked, though – he was just going through the same tinkering stage that Leonardo and the Wrights had, having fun playing with inventions. He also invented a turnspit for turning meat over when it's roasting in front of a fire – based on his cousin Daisy's sewing machine. But Daisy wasn't too happy – in fact, she made a huge fuss, so he had to uninvent it again.

In 1887, Guglielmo failed to get into the Naval Academy, annoying his dad still more, and started work at the Leghorn Technical Institute to study physics and chemistry instead. He loved it – so much so that his mum arranged extra lessons. Guglielmo was all set to be really clever but he just didn't have the track record…

The Academic Admissions Assessor
Bologna University, Bologna

Dear Mr Marconi,

I am writing to inform you that your application to the University has been turned down, because you're stupid.

Thank you for your interest in the University. Please direct it elsewhere in future.

With best wishes

Guglielmo wasn't doing too well – it's even said that because his dad wouldn't give him any money to buy equipment, he sold his shoes to pay for it. (Actually this story is rather hard to believe, and, given that Guglielmo's mum really liked him, I expect she bought him a new pair. Guglielmo isn't, on the whole, the sort of inventor you need to feel sorry for, unlike most of the others, who had some really bad moments. So put that handkerchief away.)

The handy Professor

Now there's a bit of an incredible coincidence coming up…

WHAT I NEED IS A PHYSICIST, WITH ACCESS TO A UNIVERSITY LIBRARY AND A LAB, WHO IS ALSO AN EXPERT ON HERTZ…

AH, HELLO PROFESSOR RIGHI!

Professor Augusto Righi had copied Hertz's experiments, and Mrs M talked him into seeing Guglielmo. Augusto must have liked him, because he was soon allowed to use his laboratory and the Bologna University library. There he read about what a nuisance laying a cable across the Atlantic to send telegraph signals had turned out to be. And after all the bother it still wasn't great – it was slow, expensive, needed lots of maintenance, and was no good at all for telegraphing Australia, being somewhat nobbled by the fact it didn't go there.

The telegraph was a bit like canals before George Stephenson or steam engines before James Watt: in its limited way it was absolutely brilliant, until Bell's and Edison's telephone and Marconi's radio knocked its socks off. The telephone meant words rather than blips could be transmitted, and the radio meant communication between vehicles and across seas and great distances was on the cards at last.

But Guglielmo was sure long-range radio communication was possible, and he began experiments in a secret laboratory in the attic set up by Mrs M. He set up a similar apparatus to the one that Heinrich and Augusto had used. But he was lucky in that by then a much better detector of radio waves had been developed, called the Branly coherer. It was used instead of Heinrich's spark-gap, and it worked like this:

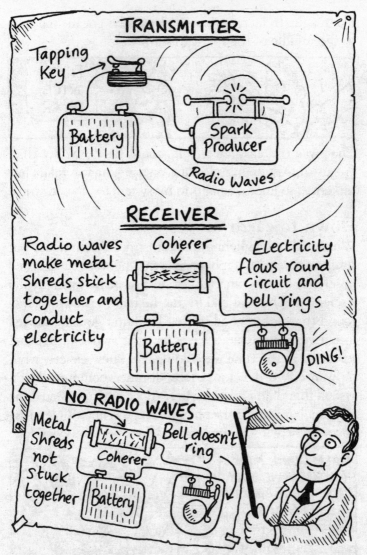

TRANSMITTER

Tapping Key

Battery

Spark Producer

Radio Waves

RECEIVER

Coherer

Radio waves make metal shreds stick together and conduct electricity

Battery

Electricity flows round circuit and bell rings

DING!

NO RADIO WAVES

Metal shreds not stuck together

Coherer

Bell doesn't ring

Battery

It wasn't long before Guglielmo was able to ring a bell by pressing a button nine metres away, with no wires between the two – in those days, it must have seemed

159

like magic. In fact, he was so pleased he got his mum up in the middle of the night to show her.

That was the easy bit – but, could he do better than Augusto? Despite his scientific training, he was really just tinkering, so improvements to his system took a long time.

Down to earth

What makes Guglielmo different from Archimedes but similar to George Stephenson is that he wasn't interested in science for its own sake – so in a sense he wasn't really a scientist. This was bad in that he had to tinker his way round things, but good in that he didn't get sidetracked into investigating radio waves for their own sake, as other scientists at the time were doing. He knew exactly what he wanted: to develop a long-distance communication system that didn't rely on wires. Aleck and Tom had done a great job inventing the phone, but it was impossible to use at sea – where it sometimes would have been very handy…

After much experimenting, he managed to increase the range of his apparatus. His dad decided there was something in Guglielmo's experiments after all, and in 1895 he gave his son some money and a big lecture on spending it wisely.

The next thing Guglielmo invented was the earth.

I'll do the jokes, thanks.

The earth was simply a connection to the ground and, combined with an aerial, it immediately increased the range of Guglielmo's radio: the aerial could pick up much weaker signals, and the connection to the Earth allowed them to flow strongly through the receiving apparatus. Guglielmo was very modest about how he invented the aerial/earth system, saying that it was just a lucky experiment – but he was so thorough in his approach, trying every possible modification to his apparatus and testing its effect, that his results were better than the most knowledgeable scientist of the time could have achieved. And that was it: the first proper radio was all invented and ready (given a bit of fiddling) to use.

Guglielmo also found that his receivers still picked up his messages – which were mostly esses because in Morse an S is three short blips, which is nice and clear and simple – even when there was a hill in the way. This was odd, really, considering what radio waves are…

Though radio waves were discovered by Heinrich Hertz, they had been predicted in 1873 by James Clerk Maxwell, who was one of the greatest scientists ever, even though he's not dead famous. He'd worked out that a radio wave is a pattern of changing electric and magnetic fields, zipping through space at the speed of light. In fact, light is just the same as radio: the only difference is the length of the wave-shape.

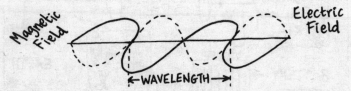

The radio waves Guglielmo was using were about a million times longer than the waves of light. But they travel in straight lines like light, so how could they cope with hills? Guglielmo didn't know, and could only assume they went through the hill. In fact, no one knew the answer until the 1920s when it was realized that it's all because of a part of the upper atmosphere called the ionosphere.

There, the sun's radiation breaks up some of the air molecules into electrically charged bits called ions. These ionized layers reflect some radio waves of certain lengths, which is very handy. It meant there was no limit to the distance radio waves could travel if the transmitter was strong enough and the receiver was sensitive enough.

By this time, Guglielmo had a system which could send messages over distances of several kilometres, even over the horizon – there was no reason why it couldn't be sent over the sea and be used wherever telegraphs couldn't. So Guglielmo wrote to the Italian Post Office to see if they were interested. They said…

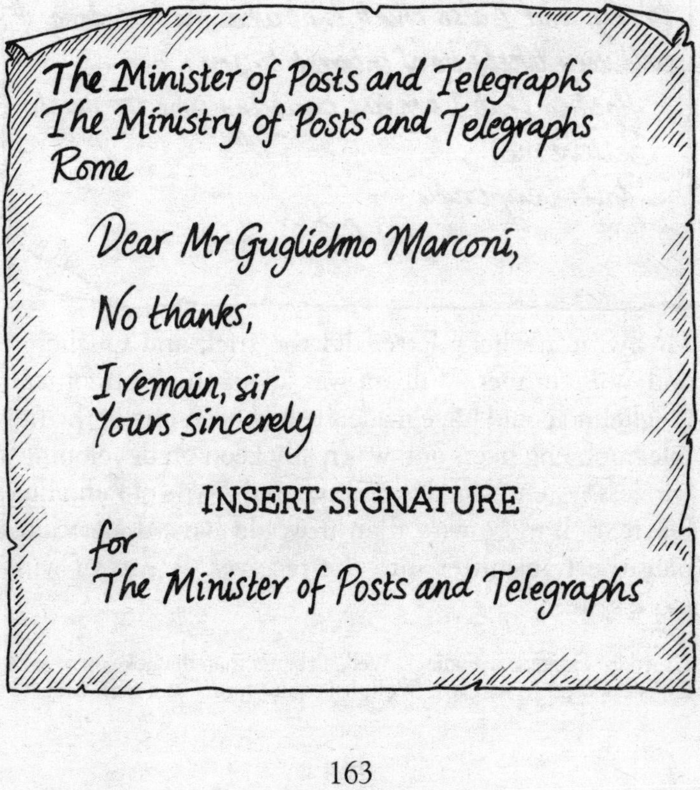

The Minister of Posts and Telegraphs
The Ministry of Posts and Telegraphs
Rome

Dear Mr Guglielmo Marconi,

No thanks,

I remain, sir
Yours sincerely

INSERT SIGNATURE

for
The Minister of Posts and Telegraphs

How annoying. However, a combination of his mum and luck came to his rescue. Mrs M was English, and she had a nephew who was an engineer. So she and Guglielmo set off to England, and the nephew helped Guglielmo coax his equipment back into working order after the customs people had fiddled about with it. He then introduced Guglielmo to a friend of his who wrote a rather grovelly sort of letter to William Preece, chief engineer to the Post Office. The letter ended:

> *It has occurred to me that you might possibly be kind enough to see him and hear what he has to say, and I also think that what he has done will very likely be of interest to you.*
>
> *Hoping that I am not troubling you too much. Believe me*
>
> *Yours very truly*
>
> *A A C Swinton*

Mr Swinton's licky letter did the trick and Guglielmo and William met. William was about the best contact[1] Guglielmo could have made: he had been one of the first telegraph engineers and was really keen on developing a wireless system – he'd even invented a type of radio link, but it took more wire than it would have done to just plug the transmitter into the receiver. A sort of wire-more system.[2]

1. Geddit? Contact ... radio... Well, it's better than that joke on page 24.
2. As opposed to wire*less*. Well, it is quite funny in a way. Isn't it?

FROM: GUGLIELMO, GENERAL POST OFFICE, LONDON
TO: MUM, BAYSWATER, LONDON
DATE: 31 MARCH 1896
WILLIAM PREECE THINKS WIRELESS KNOCKOUT. KEEN TO
SAVE LIVES AT SEA. ME TOO. SO THINKS ME KNOCKOUT
TOO.

FROM: GUGLIELMO, GENERAL POST OFFICE, LONDON
TO: MUM, BAYSWATER, LONDON
DATE: 27 JULY 1896
FIRST PUBLIC DEMONSTRATION OF WIRELESS, ACROSS
ONE MILE OF LONDON. ALL PLEASED. WORE GREEN TIE.[1]

FROM: GUGLIELMO, SALISBURY PLAIN, WILTSHIRE
TO: MUM, BAYSWATER, LONDON
DATE: 2 SEPTEMBER 1896
JUST SENT WIRELESS MESSAGE OVER A MILE ACROSS
SALISBURY PLAIN. BLOKES FROM POST OFFICE, ARMY
AND NAVY ALL HAPPY. STRIPY TIE TODAY. BECAME DEAD
FAMOUS.

FROM: GUGLIELMO, TOYNBEE HALL, LONDON
TO: MUM, LONDON
DATE: 12 DECEMBER 1896
WILLIAM AND I GAVE PUBLIC LECTURE. I CARRIED
ELECTRIC BELL. WILLIAM RANG IT BY WIRELESS. SPOTTY
TIE. ALL LOVED IT, ALSO DEMO.

1. Guglielmo was always intensely stylish. After all, he was Italian.

An essless message

By now Guglielmo realized that the main thing that limited the range of the radio signals was the aerial, so he developed better ones. By 1897 he could send signals more than 14 kilometres, and he realized he was really going places, so he formed the Wireless Telegraph Company, which later became the Marconi Company and will become John Logie Baird's rival.

By this time, the Italian government was feeling a bit sorry for itself, and asked him if he wouldn't mind coming home. Fortunately, Guglielmo didn't bear any grudges, so he went back to Italy and in July he tried sending a signal from a ship to the shore. There was a nasty moment when Guglielmo found he had nothing to support his aerial with, but he found a broom, stuck his aerial to it and talked someone into holding it in the air just in time. To show he forgave Italy, he transmitted 'Viva l'Italia' instead of 'S' for a change.

Over the next few years Guglielmo increased the range of his radio waves. He sent them across the Channel in 1899, and the same year he went to the USA, where his invention saved a life for the first time, when someone fell overboard at a yacht race. He also made a vital development by working out how to tune radios.

The idea of tuning was the key to Aleck's harmonic telegraph, and it's easy to see why it's essential for radio. If there are several local radio transmitters in operation, the receivers will pick up all their signals at once, unless there's a way for the receiver to select just one signal. The answer is to make the signals different, by sending them on different frequencies. This is what people do too – to make yourself heard in a crowd, you sometimes unconsciously change the pitch of your voice so that it's different from other people's (if you're too polite to shout that is). Another advantage of tuning is that it saves a lot of power.

Guglielmo's fun ban

Sending radio messages across the Atlantic was the obvious next dramatic thing for Guglielmo to do. But this one was really tricky. He set up a massive ring of masts in Poldhu on the Cornish coast and, because he wanted a two-way radio link, another one at Cape Cod in the United States. The rings were 61 m high, 61 m across, very dramatic and a bit pricey. But they both blew down in gales before they could be used.

Guglielmo cobbled together a replacement aerial at Poldhu and, in Cape Cod, he settled for two kites and a balloon. The balloon and one of the kites blew away, but he used the other kite to get the signal he wanted – he cabled Poldhu to send his favourite message, 'S', and finally, despite another gale, he heard it.

EXCUSE ME, BUT COULD YOU DO ME A FAVOUR?

Not everyone believed Guglielmo (though Edison did and said so, loudly) but further demonstrations convinced them, especially once Guglielmo invented a machine to print out the Morse messages radio receivers picked up, so people didn't have to rely on someone straining their ears to make out bips and bleeps through interference.

Because the ionosphere still hadn't been discovered, no one could really understand how Guglielmo had done it: you can't see America from England because the Earth gets in the way. Since radio waves are like light waves people didn't see how they could get across the Atlantic if light couldn't.

But never mind: from then on, all Guglielmo really had to do was sit back and watch his dreams come true. He was rich and famous and, what was very important to him, his radio was saving lives at sea – 1,700 people were rescued from shipwreck in 1909, thanks to a radio message, and it was radio that saved many of the *Titanic*'s passengers in 1912. Many more would have survived if the radio operator on a nearby ship hadn't been off duty at the crucial moment.

Radio communication had a few teething troubles of course – for instance, sometimes when there was lots of interference, early Morse printers would print out extra dots – which are 'e's in Morse...

MESSAGE READS: "PLEEEASE HEELP. I AM BEEEEEING ATTACKEEEED BY KILLEER BEEEE-EEEEEEEEEES.

In 1905, Guglielmo got married to posh-but-poor Beatrice O'Brien, and a very jealous husband he turned out to be, hardly letting her out of the house without him in case she smiled at other blokes, which was odd really, because marriage didn't stop him having girlfriends. But he and Beatrice stayed married until 1924 and they had four children.

Radio gave Guglielmo a great life: he received the Nobel Prize (an international annual award for top scientists) in 1909, he became a diplomat, he was matey with Tom Edison and Aleck Bell and he had so much money he was able to live just as he liked. He'd always loved the sea, so 'just as he liked' meant living in a ship with his friends and family, having huge parties for royals and listening to the radio.

So it was wall-to-wall fun from then on... Or it should have been, but, to be honest, Guglielmo wasn't a very laid-back kind of a person. He insisted that his meals were timed to the second, he showed little emotion at his successes and failures, he complained if he had to wait for lifts to arrive and he hated sharing them when they did.

So, being a bit on the tense and snappy side, it's not surprising that, according to some biographers, Guglielmo didn't think the radio was for enjoying yourself with. In fact his company is supposed to have lost lots of money because he didn't let it get involved in entertainment broadcasting. What radio *wasn't* for was fun – this was a serious invention, not for messing about with. Of course, there is a limit to how much entertainment you can get from listening to Morse code, but since 1902 it had been possible to send anything by radio...

I *mean* any signal – like words, music, or chat-shows. There were plenty of people who were determined to use radio for just that sort of frivolity – like the BBC, for instance, which had been formed in 1922 from the Marconi Company and others. Once it was OK to have fun with them, everyone loved radios. One of early radio's first big moments was in 1920 when Nelly Melba, a famous opera singer, gave a concert from the Marconi studios in Chelmsford that could be received thousands of kilometres away. When the engineer told her that her voice would be broadcast from the top of the 135 metre-high aerial masts, she peered up at them and said…

Young man, if you think I am going to climb up there you are greatly mistaken.

Presumably Guglielmo was *not* amused by all this frivolity and wild entertainment.

Guglielmo was also intensely patriotic, no matter what Italy did, and in 1923 he joined the Italian Fascist Party, which – well, which was just horrible, really. The Fascists believed in absolute state control, and in taking people's rights away. When, in 1935, the Fascist government prepared to attack Abyssinia (now Ethiopia) lots of the world's governments protested. Marconi went off on a world tour to speak up for Italy.

World Wide Wireless

As Guglielmo got older, the radio waves he liked got shorter. The advantages of shorter waves are that they need shorter aerials, use less power, and are more directional. By 1926 there were several stations around the world transmitting short-wave radio messages to each other. The design of Guglielmo's short-wave transmitters was so good that 40 years later when the

Science Museum asked for a clapped-out one, it was told there weren't any – they were all still working!

But Guglielmo was also interested in shorter waves still, waves which are now called microwaves. He did some early experiments showing that metal objects could be tracked by the effect they had on these waves – experiments that might have led to radar. But Guglielmo didn't live to finish them. He died in 1937, and there was a two-minute radio silence all over the world.

Guglielmo knew that radio was amazing, but when he once said that he could use it to see through walls, he was only joking. (He told the reporter not to tell anyone, so it was in *all* the papers the next day). He couldn't really do it.

BUT I CAN

GUGLIELMO MARCONI
THAT WAS YOUR LIFE

TOP INVENTIONS:
- radio transmissions over useful distances
- aerial/earth system
- worldwide radio communications network

ALSO DEAD FAMOUS FOR:
starting the Marconi Company

JOHN LOGIE BAIRD
AND HIS SPINNING TELLY

CAMPBELL SWINTON[1] INVENTS TELEVISION

ROSING INVENTS TELEVISION

BAIRD INVENTS TELEVISION

JENKINS INVENTS TELEVISION

VON MIHALY INVENTS TELEVISION

RIGNOUX & FOURNIER INVENT TELEVISION

ZWORKIN INVENTS TV!

DIECKMANN INVENTS TV!

FARNSWORTH INVENTS TV!

TAKAYANAGI INVENTS TELEVISION

So who really did it? Well, in a way, they all did. Like the flying machine, television was something that people had struggled to invent for ages. It was such a lovely idea, and it seemed so simple: Aleck Bell had learned to send voices through wires, couldn't someone do the same thing with pictures? Or even send them through

1. That's the bloke who wrote the letter on page 164.

the air, as Guglielmo had with Morse signals? Also, people had been going to the cinema since the 1890s, so the idea of moving pictures wasn't new. But unlike TV, cinema is no good for showing things to millions of people simultaneously, transmitting live action or watching in daylight.

Moving pictures

A cinema film projector works quite differently from a television: in a cinema, a beam of light shines though a moving strip of film on to which images have been printed, much like a Kinetoscope (see page 105), except the beam of light is used to project a moving picture on to a wall instead of in to someone's eyes. A television set works by sending a ray of light or a beam of electrons scuttling all over a screen, which glows in response. The light or the electron beam changes in strength really, really rapidly, drawing a new picture on the screen many times a second. The way the light ray or electron beam changes is usually controlled by a radio signal from the TV transmitter.

A television system's job is to change light to electricity and back to light again: the image of the thing being televised is converted to an electrical signal, which is transmitted through space to the television set, which converts the signal back to an image again. This is a little bit like what Aleck did with sound, but it's a lot more tricky: a sound is just a signal that changes over time in frequency (which we hear as pitch) and in strength (which we call loudness). It's easy to make an electrical signal change in frequency and strength in the same way as a sound signal.

Light isn't so different from sound: it also varies in frequency (which we see as colour) and strength (which we see as brightness), so we could fairly easily transmit this information by an electrical signal, and change it back into light at the other end. All we'd need is something like a microphone, but which changes its resistance in response to changes in light instead of changes in sound.

But there's more to a picture than colour and brightness – a TV picture all of one colour and brightness might not be terribly useful, though possibly rather arty. Different bits of a picture have different colours and brightnesses, so it seems as if the signal corresponding to it would have to contain thousands of different frequencies and strengths all at the same time. It's as if Bell had to invent a telephone that could transmit thousands of voices at once, so that they could all be heard separately.

Now does it sound easy? Let's see how John Logie Baird did it.

A crash and a bang

John was born in 1888 in an old-fashioned house on the north-west coast of Scotland. It was a lot less old-fashioned, though, when John had sorted it out. First of all, he built a telephone exchange so that he and his friends could ring each other up. It actually worked very well – Aleck would have been proud of his fellow-Scotsman. Sadly though, the wires were a bit low and hung over the road and one day...

So John had to take his wires down again. He soon found another use for them though, and within a few weeks, the house was the only one for miles with electric light – powered by a generator under the kitchen sink. Tom Edison would have been proud of that.

Poor John wasn't a terribly fit bloke – in fact he never really recovered from an attack of bronchitis he had when he was two. This was actually just as well for TV though, as we'll see. Being a bit frail didn't stop him trying to fly: he built a glider with a friend, and flew in it too, for about two seconds. After which...

The Wright brothers wouldn't have been proud of that.

So John reckoned conquering the air wasn't for him, particularly considering the Wright brothers had done it already. We don't know when he really got going on the idea of inventing TV, but he was certainly doing related experiments by 1903, when he was 15. He was trying to solve the first problem of television: how do you change light into electricity?

Now, this question had been half-answered 30 years before, when it was discovered that a metal called selenium has the odd property that its resistance to electricity changes depending on the amount of light that falls on it. So it should be possible to make something like a light-microphone, giving an electrical signal that changed in response to the amount of light present, as the signal from a microphone changes in response to the amount of sound present.

SO THAT'S TELLY SORTED, THEN!

Well, sadly, no. Selenium couldn't be obtained in a very pure form at the time, which meant that the effect was very small. It also took quite a while to react to changes of light: far too slowly to use in a TV as it was. John found out for himself the problems with selenium when he first started trying to build TV systems, maybe as early as 1912 – but no one is too sure of the details because he was quite secretive and scared of his ideas being pinched. Later there were other reasons for secrecy.

John wasn't terribly good at practical things, but he did his best. While he was doing a course at the Royal

Technical College in Glasgow, he was also working with engineering firms to get some practical experience, so he'd know all about exciting new technology and state-of-the-art industrial processing and modern business methods.

John didn't give up trying to invent things. Like diamonds. He reckoned he could do it, given some carbon and a lot of electrical power. It wasn't a completely daft idea, since diamonds *are* made of carbon. The good news was he had plenty of electricity, since he was working for the Glasgow Electricity Company at the time. The bad news was...

HALF OF GLASGOW BLACKED OUT IN POWER-CUT. MAD BOFFIN'S DIAMOND-MAKING ATTEMPT FAILS. JOBLESS TOTAL UP BY ONE.

Very annoying. So he decided to—

No. He concentrated on selling something he'd invented already...

Supersocks

John's invention was proudly named: *THE BAIRD UNDERSOCK*. In fact, it wasn't all that brilliant – it was just a sock with a bit of powder on to keep it dry and hence snuggly. The powder would have melted away the first time the socks were washed, so it was a choice between smelly snuggly feet or fragrant frozen ones. But what was clever was how John advertised his socks: he got women to wear big sandwich-boards which said...

It was unheard of for women to do this, and he, they, and the socks became famous. In fact, he made quite a bit of money out of them. Another clever move was to get his friends to ring up shops demanding more socks, thereby generating an out-of-stock sock shock in the shops. So John had found he was good at marketing which, as we've seen before, is a vital skill to get an invention off the ground, even if it's not a flying machine. Sadly, he had one of his terrible colds and the sock business folded, much like the socks.

Something startling in your sandwich

So, what would he do? His frequent colds were really getting on his nerves, and, like Aleck Bell's parents, he decided that Scotland was to blame, so he left – but not for America. He went to Trinidad to sell cotton.

WHAT DID THEY WANT COTTON FOR IN TRINIDAD?

Actually, nothing. So, since Trinidad is packed with fruit, John tried making jam instead. But Trinidad also has lots of insects, all of whom like a bit of jam for their tea. Or anytime really. So instead of raspberry or plum jam, John ended up with flavours like…

GUAVA & GRUB CRAWLY CURD LOGAN-BERRY & LOUSE SCORPION SURPRISE

Which no one really liked, except insects. John didn't mind them too much – he even kept a particularly gigantic locust as a pet, but it scuppered his jam-making attempts, since even he didn't like them on toast. All his marketing skills couldn't make the jam sell, even when he'd fished most of the insects out. So he went home the next year.

Speedy soap and shocking shoes

Back in London, he thought he'd have a go at soap-selling, but he was a bit sick of inventing everything himself and, having discovered with his socks that he was good at selling things, he just bought some cheap soap, called it 'Baird's Speedy Cleaner' and sold it for a higher price.

Yet again, all was going well for a while, until he got a terrible cold and had to stop working. In despair, he sold his company to a rival called Hutchinson who'd brought out 'Rapid Washer' soap in competition with 'Speedy Cleaner', and went to the south coast. He decided it really was about time that he settled down and invented…

No, the pneumatic (air-filled) shoe. They'd be ever so bouncy and comfy, but sadly, the prototype pair went POP on their first outing. Other inventions didn't do well either – his pile cream (which wasn't his really – it was a recipe one of his work-mates gave him) made him itchy and he cut himself with his rustless razor (because it was made of glass). So John decided he might as well try inventing…

Nope…

Teeeeeeeeeeeeee… V!

After much messing about, he ended up with a working version. Sadly it's not exactly certain what it looked like or how it worked. It has to be said that we're a bit in the dark about *exactly* how any of John's televisions worked, because he was so secretive about them. It also has to be said that today's tellies have got absolutely nothing in common with John's. His was an entirely mechanical system, but today's are electronic. While John was working away, others were developing electronic versions of TV. It's true that John's mechanical system could never have achieved the results we have today, however sophisticated it had become – but in the early 1920s electronics just wasn't up to producing a working TV at all. So John didn't use electronics – he used coffin-wood, a hatbox, bits of old bike and some darning needles!

Watching John's first TV was a bit like watching an oblong a few square centimetres in area which flickered and flashed in black and a single shade of pink. There wasn't much in the way of programmes either.

Because exactly when John did this is uncertain, it's also uncertain whether he was first or not. Certainly, very similar things were being done about then in the U.S.

After a while, John's landlord got a bit sick of him turning his room into a lab full of bits of telly and threw him out. Now rather healthier, he set off back to London where he didn't do too well with accommodation either – he was asked to leave one lodgings partly because he spent mealtimes making weird faces in the mirror, a bit like Aleck Bell used to. His TV projects had their problems too, though he managed to get an interview with Guglielmo's company to try to sell them the idea of television. The interview started like this…

…and went downhill from there. Ironically enough, the Marconi Company got really into TV soon after, and John found, to his irritation, that a lot of people thought Guglielmo himself had invented it.

But the next couple of things John did definitely were world-firsts. In April 1925 he managed to get some more publicity – and money – by demonstrating his TV at Selfridges. He scared shoppers silly with terrifying masks that winked at them.

(Some of the shoppers scared John back, by nearly electrocuting themselves fiddling with the wires.) And then…

❧ JOHN LOGIE BAIRD'S ❧
SECRET TV TIMES

2 October 1925

10:00 am: The Dummy Ventriloquist's dummy Stookie Bill stars in a short TV show, brought to you NOT just in boring old black-and-pink, but, for the first time, in a whole dazzling range of colours. Light pink, dark pink, pink so dim it's almost black, whatever pink you like, it's on your TV today (if your name's John Logie Baird).

11:00 am: The Boy on the Box
William Taynton stars in the first ever television show to star a human being. William, who was employed as an office boy until this opportunity knocked, said 'I only did it 'cos he gave me two and six. Can I go now, please?'

11:10 am: Closedown

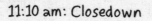

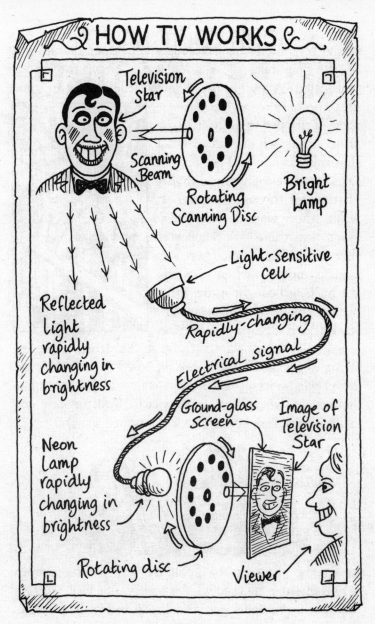

Only a few months later, in January 1926, John was ready to publicize his TV properly, by demonstrating it to the members of a scientific society, the Royal Institution. About 40 people attended, but not in some plush hotel or shiny laboratory – they all trooped up to John's tiny London flat, which was so small that they couldn't all get into it. Luckily there were three flights of stairs for the rest to stand on while they waited. John also made sure there was a reporter there, from *The Times*. There was a tricky moment when someone got his beard caught in the telly, but otherwise it went very well. In fact, the Royal Institution

loved it – they all wanted to be on TV. It was great fun trying to guess who they were supposed to be looking at. *The Times* reporter did his bit too, and John became famous as The Television Man (which fortunately was much easier than being The Renaissance Man).

In a way, this sort of publicity was John's greatest achievement – he made TV a reality, not by inventing it, but by convincing everyone that it was really possible.

Terror TV

Of course, like George's trains, Aleck's phones and Archimedes' Claw, some people were a bit nervous of this new invention. People thought if they could see someone on TV, that person could see them. Some even thought TV could read their thoughts. But they were safer than trains, and *much* safer than The Claw, and they had guards round the spinning bits so you couldn't catch your beard in them, should you be equipped with one. Mind you, some of the experimental ones *were* a bit dangerous: some of the spinning discs were eight feet in diameter, full of bits of glass, and spun round two-and-a-half times a second. Sometimes the glass lenses would pop out, as John said...

> *...striking the walls or roof like bomb shells. The apparatus would then get out of balance and jump from one side of the lab to the other until it was stopped or the disc tore itself to pieces.*

Other experiments included using a dead person's eye in place of a camera (John abandoned this even quicker than Aleck abandoned his dead person's ear machine), and making a TV camera that would work in complete darkness. This was quite successful: instead of light, it used heat. When the British Association of Science came to a demonstration of this invention, there were such huge crowds that police had to clear them. The only trouble was, whoever was being televised got very hot, and one of them burst into flames. Fortunately it was only one of John's puppets, but it put people off a bit, and the idea never really caught on.

By this time – 1927 – John had lots of competition. Aleck's company was working on TV by now, and in April they sent a television image down a phone line from Washington to New York (which is over 300 kilometres). The next month, John sent one from London to Glasgow, which was more than twice as far, so there. By this time John, with his former rival George Hutchinson (the 'Rapid Washer' man) and some daring stockbrokers, had formed a company. Since the company depended completely on John and his cleverness, his life was insured for £150,000 – which was then the highest policy ever taken out on a human being. John wasn't too keen on the company's chairman who was the chairman of lots of other companies too, smoked huge cigars and was very fat. He used to come and bother John in his lab with silly suggestions until John made a specially narrow door to keep him out.

Phone lines weren't ideal ways to send pictures, and in February 1928 John sent a TV signal by radio from

London to Hartsdale, near New York. People compared the event to Marconi's first transatlantic message 27 years earlier, but it wasn't an S that was sent this time, but someone called Mia Howe. Another signal – someone called Dora – was sent from London to a ship 1,600 kilometres out at sea. Soon after, the first TVs, which John called televisors, went on sale – though not many people bought them, since they cost several months' wages, and there wasn't much to watch.

In England, the BBC was the obvious organization to make TV programmes to watch on these expensive tellies. The head of the BBC, John Reith, wasn't keen on the idea of TV at all, and wasn't very helpful. But, after a lot of argy-bargy and also some work with the BBC's rival, the German Broadcasting Company, John started to send his broadcasts in 1929, though only for half an hour each weekday, in the middle of the night.

The broadcasts included plays, interviews, performing animals and, on one occasion, some workmen swearing and singing dodgy songs, when someone had accidentally left the transmitter switched on. The papers next day had headlines like 'Mysterious Vulgar Broadcast'.

It was a good year for John – he also invented and demonstrated colour TV[1], 3-D TV and video recording.

1. A version of colour TV was patented in 1904, using a system of electrical sparks that shone through red, blue and yellow filters. The inventor was a Mr Frankenstein.

He often wore odd shoes and socks too, and a scruffy checked jacket that Guglielmo wouldn't have been seen dead in, but never mind, eh?

Slight technical difficulties

So why aren't we using John's TVs now? Because, to be perfectly honest, the quality of the picture was complete pants. It was all flickery and indistinct and very small. John would have been the first to admit this, but he knew it was just the start. The public knew about the poor quality too, thanks to all the publicity, but that didn't put them off a bit, any more than Aleck's phones being a bit hard to hear down did. Perhaps the fact that hardly anyone could afford one helped.

In those days, watching TV was a bit weird and being on TV was a bit tiring since the pictures and sound were sent at different times. Say you're a famous Italian tenor, and you want to be a TV celeb...

This sort of thing put some people off being TV stars, but others, liking a challenge and the chance to say 'That's Showbiz!', were quite keen. In March 1930, however, the BBC did finally allow *two* radio frequencies to be assigned to a TV show, so one could be used for sound and the other for pictures, both at the same time. This was an exciting moment and famous actors, personalities, celebrities, stars and Gracie Fields (ask your granny) flocked in from all over the place to be televised.

Over the next few years, John invented loads of new tellies and showed all sorts of things on them.

Battle of the tellies

While John was concentrating on impressing people with his amazing mechanical televisions, research into electronic television was catching up. By the mid-1930s the government decided there really was something in this television thing and it had better make its mind up what to do about it. By then there were two main types of TV around in Britain: an electronic system developed by the Marconi-EMI companies, and John's mechanical system (or mostly mechanical – John had built some electronics into it by then). A committee was appointed to decide which was best, and after a year of coffee drinking and chatting it announced its decision. Which was that it wasn't really sure. The committee decided the only way to find out was to try both systems out on people (which was a good idea, though I'm not sure why it took a year to come up with).

So, from 2 November 1936 programmes were transmitted by the two systems on alternate evenings.

At the time, tellies still cost as much as cars. So it was just as well they could accept either type of signal, so people wouldn't need two TVs each, of which one would soon be useless.

So what could the people who'd spent enormous sums watch on the two hours per day (except Sundays) when there was anything on?

TELEVISOR TIMES

3 November 1936

3:00 pm: Someone reading this out.

3:05 pm: Some Alsatians, plus a man to describe them.

3:15 pm: News.

3:25 pm: Mr Stock tells us about his model of a ship.

3:40 pm: Little break to get over the excitement generated by the model ship, PLUS: the time (which will be 3:40 pm).

3:45 pm: Two film stars, one of whom may sing a song. Or, then again, not.

4:00 pm: A chart arranged in cooperation with the Air Ministry, will forecast the weather.

9:00 pm - 10:00 pm: Exactly the same as 3:00 pm - 4:00 pm except the two film stars are replaced by a Spanish dancer.

In November 1937, the committee agreed that the winner was … not John. Though it was superior in some ways – for transmitting pre-recorded film, for instance –

his system was too flickery, too grainy and had less development potential than the all-electronic system.

John wasn't happy at all. It wasn't a financial disaster because his company was doing well making television receivers, but it was terribly depressing. He returned to the use of TV in cinemas and kept developing his systems.

Then in 1939, the Second World War began, and all TV transmissions were stopped. There was a good reason for the switch-off: German bombers could easily have used TV transmissions as if they were big 'Drop Bomb Here' signs, simply by homing in on the signals. Baird Television Ltd went out of business, but John was still busy, working on secret projects for the war office, like flying TV…

…a TV camera carried in a French bomber, actually, and probably night-vision, radar and high-speed signalling (back in Trinidad, oddly enough). He wasn't completely wrapped up in his work though – one day he was staying with some friends outside London to avoid air-raids, but went back in again to get a 'vital piece of equipment' – which turned out to be his kitten.

He also entertained his kids with fluffy animal stories. Well, sort of. They actually starred a family of houseflies and were all about the horrible food they had to eat and how it made them really ill.

As the war went on, John's house got more and more blown up until he couldn't live there any more, but he went on developing new forms of TV there. He soon had a new company too – Cinema Television – and he developed new sorts of TV, including all-electronic, 3-D, colour and large-screen versions. But before long, John was ill again. He thought it was one of his usual terrible colds, but this time he didn't recover, and he died in 1946, soon after TV transmissions had started up again. His TV research was abandoned, including his latest 3-D telly. We still haven't got one to work properly.

JOHN LOGIE BAIRD
THAT WAS YOUR LIFE

TOP INVENTIONS:
• working mechanical television system
• colour television
• 3-D television

ALSO DEAD FAMOUS FOR:
being 'The Television Man'

INVENTORS 'R' US

You'll have noticed that it's not always easy to say just who invented what, and that hardly anything was invented by just one person. But that's not to say there are no individual inventors any more – there's Trevor Baylis who invented the clockwork radio, and James Dyson who invented the bagless vacuum cleaner.

So if you want to be an inventor – maybe the first dead famous female inventor – what do you do?

As we've seen lots of times, it's not enough (in fact it's not even necessary) to come up with a brilliantly original idea. A successful invention just has to be something that people will really want: ideally something that they don't know they want. Give them that and you'll be a success – so long as you protect yourself by patenting your invention. Without patents, Tom Edison, Aleck Bell, Guglielmo Marconi and most other inventors would have got nowhere.

Also, though a good scientific training will give you a lot more chance of success, it's not essential. There are several sorts of inventors in this book: some who worked by trial and error like George Stephenson; some who worked out the answers logically, like James Watt; and some who put together earlier ideas and used the latest technology to make them work, like John Logie Baird. So:

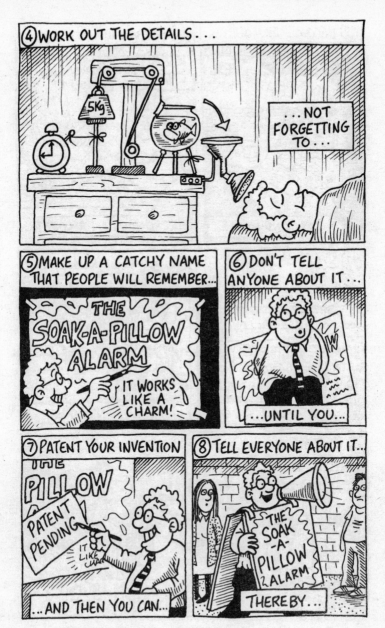

So, what might you invent? Some of the inventors in this book invented things which everyone already wanted – like television or planes. So you could invent somthing that people really want, like:
• cures for everything from colds to cancer
• a nice light high-capacity rechargeable battery
• a way to cancel out noise so people can listen to music as loud as they like without bothering anyone else
• self-fertilizing crops to feed the world
• a pain reliever with no side effects
• a superconductor than works at room temperature so a lot less electricity is wasted
• an intelligent robot
• a way of neutralizing nuclear waste
• 3-D television
• a substitute for wood so we don't run out of forests.

Of course, all these things are being worked on by big businesses or universities. But if you don't fancy competing with them – or joining them – you could always come up with an amazing thing that people always wanted without knowing it, like the phonograph.

Then you'd be dead famous, just like…

DEAD FAMOUS INVENTIONS: WHEELS TO STARSHIPS IN EASY-TO-SWALLOW CHUNKS

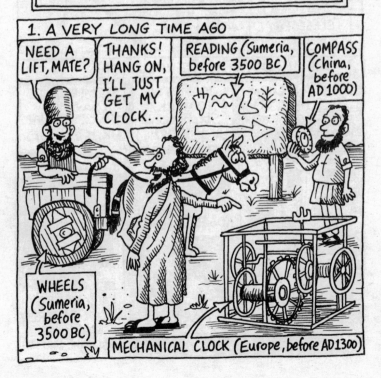

1. A VERY LONG TIME AGO

NEED A LIFT, MATE?

THANKS! HANG ON, I'LL JUST GET MY CLOCK...

READING (Sumeria, before 3500 BC)

COMPASS (China, before AD 1000)

WHEELS (Sumeria, before 3500 BC)

MECHANICAL CLOCK (Europe, before AD 1300)